# MEL BAY'S
# ANTHOLOGY OF PEDAL STEEL GUITAR
## E9 CHROMATIC TUNING
## BY
# DeWitt Scott

## OTHER ARTISTS

| Tune | Steel Player |
|---|---|
| Hot Foot | Weldon Myrick |
| Brown Baggin' | Mike Smith |
| Russian Rolls | Nils Tuxen |
| Blue Jade | Buddy Emmons |
| Song For Sara | Paul Franklin |
| Londonderry Aire | Buddy Emmons |
| Leather Britches | Doug Jernigan |
| Doug's Melody | Doug Jernigan |
| Reminiscing (No sound track) | Jerry Byrd |
| Bars of Steel | Lloyd Green |
| Edited by | DeWitt Scott |
| | Russ Wever |
| Recorded by | Michael Scott Productions |
| Mixed Down | Technisonic Studios |

## CREDITS

| | |
|---|---|
| Steel Guitar | DeWitt Scott |
| Steel Guitar | Russ Wever |
| Steel Guitar | Pat Heller |
| Rhythm Guitar | Don Hall |
| Bass | Ron Griggs |
| Drums | Fred Pierce |
| Front Cover | Jim Hall |

## SPECIAL MENTION

| | |
|---|---|
| George Lewis | Nashville, TN |
| Bill Atkinson | St. Louis, MO |

*Without their help years ago, I would not have the knowledge to write this book.*

DEDICATED TO MY WIFE Mary Helen

3 1336 05856 8859

A recording of the music in this book is now available. The publisher strongly recommends the use of this recording along with the text to insure accuracy of interpretation and ease in learning.

© 1980 BY MEL BAY PUBLICATIONS, INC., PACIFIC, MO 63069.
ALL RIGHTS RESERVED. INTERNATIONAL COPYRIGHT SECURED. B.M.I. MADE AND PRINTED IN U.S.A.
*Visit us on the Web at http://www.melbay.com — E-mail us at email@melbay.com*

# CONTENTS

Page

1 Credits

2 Contents

4 Description of the Steel

4 How to Select Your Steel

5 Types of Steels

6 Setting Up the Steel

7 Tuning Chart

8 Tuning to the Piano

10 Tuning to the Korg

11 Right and Left Hand Positions

12 Tab Instruction and Timing

13 Gliss or Slides

14 Finger and Timing Exercise

15 Warm Up Exercise

16 C Major Scales

17 Blocking Exercise

18 Twinkle Steel

19 Twinkle Steel in Harmony

20 Go Tell Aunt Rhody

21 Go Tell Aunt Rhody

22 Goodnight Ladies

23 Skip To My Lou

24 Single Note Pickin'

25 Fast Finger Exercise

26 Use of the Third Pedal

27 B and C Pedal

28 The Bee Cee Swing

29 Intros Mixing the ABC Pedals

Page

30 Run #1, #2, #3, Waltz Time

31 Mississippi Waltz

32 The Old "F" Knee Lever

33 The "D" Knee Lever

35 The Doodle Bug Rock

36 Doodle Bug Runs #1 and #2

37 Doodle Bug Rock With New Runs

38 G Knee Lever

39 More About G Knee Lever

40 Red River Valley

41 Runs-Licks-Fills

42 Aura Lee

43 Moveable Major Scale

44 My Bonnie Lies Over the Ocean

45 C Scale Harmonized

46 Old Black Joe

48 Silent Night

50 Sounds of Dobro

51 Dobro Sounds

52 1950's Rock

53 Boogie Woogie

54 "A" Pedal Swing

55 Western Swing Ride

56 Recognizable Intros

57 A Snappy Intro

58 The Banjo Roll

60 My Old Kentucky Home

Page

62 Silent Night

63 Marines Hymn

64 Little Liza Jane

68 Pedal Drag

70 Waltz of the Yukon

76 Amazing Grace

80 Ozark Ramble

84 Greensleeves

87 Fast Finger Exercises

88 Fast Picking

89 A Very Good Run

90 Londonderry Aire (Buddy Emmons)

96 Bars of Steel (Lloyd Green)

102 Brown Baggin' (Mike Smith)

112 Hot Foot (Weldon Myrick)

118 Russian Rolls (Nils Tuxen) [from Denmark]

122 Leather Bridges (Doug Jernigan)

128 Doug's Melody

134 Song for Sara (Paul Franklin)

140 Reminiscing (Jerry Byrd)

146 Blue Jade (Buddy Emmons)

152 Steel Guitar Magazines, News and Clubs

152 Steel Guitar Instruction

152 Steel Guitar Colleges

153 Steel Guitar Convention

153 Steel Guitar Albums

*Jerry Byrd—Master of Touch and Tone*

*Buddy Emmons—World's Foremost Steel Guitarist*

# THE PEDAL STEEL GUITAR

*Single Neck Ten Strings with Three Floor and Four Knee Levers*

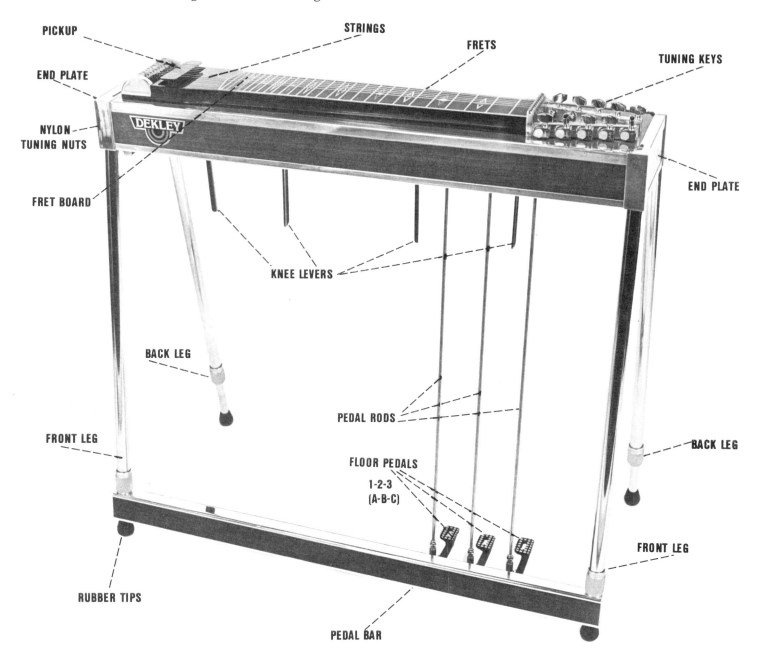

PICKUP · STRINGS · FRETS · TUNING KEYS · END PLATE · NYLON TUNING NUTS · FRET BOARD · KNEE LEVERS · BACK LEG · PEDAL RODS · FRONT LEG · FLOOR PEDALS 1-2-3 (A-B-C) · BACK LEG · FRONT LEG · RUBBER TIPS · PEDAL BAR

# HOW TO SELECT YOUR STEEL

Most steel guitar manufacturers make a student model. When you buy one; you should know the limitations that some student models have. The lower priced models are designed to at least get you started with ten strings, three floor pedals and one knee lever. This type of steel is limited because it is not designed to add any pedals or knee levers later. When you have progressed to where you need more knee levers, it's time to trade it in.

Other student model steels that cost more can accommodate more knee levers when you need them. All the steel guitars are rod operated now and all have very fine pickups on them.

On the pro models—they are all good. It's a matter of your choice and the money you want to spend *and* who has influenced you. You may want a brand name because your favorite steel player plays that brand. No matter which steel you choose, you will be spending a lot of happy hours practicing. Remember two things:

1. There is no easy way to play the steel guitar. You must practice.
2. The instrument is virtually unlimited in what it can do. Its only limit is the person playing it. Hawaiian, Country, Pop, Jazz, Classical, Rock—it's up to you!

# SHOULD YOU LEARN TO READ?

Yes! Almost every top name steel player can read music and those that can't wish they could. Have you heard this old saying, "Do you read music? —Not so much that it hurts my playing." A lot can be said about the "ear" players, but if you ever get the opportunity to learn to read music—do it!

# TYPES OF STEEL GUITARS

Pro Type versus Student Models and Economy Model

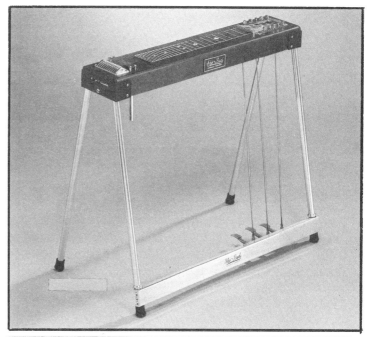

## Student Model

The student model is a single neck, ten string steel guitar and usually has three floor pedals and one knee lever. It is ideal for the beginner as it is low in cost and is limited only by the knee lever. Usually you cannot add any knee levers.

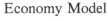

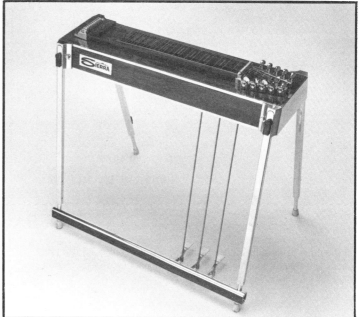

## Economy Model

This model is very versatile as additional knee levers can be added as needed. All manufacturers give you the option of adding the additional knee levers when you first purchase the guitar. I would recommend that you purchase one that has three floor pedals and three knee levers.

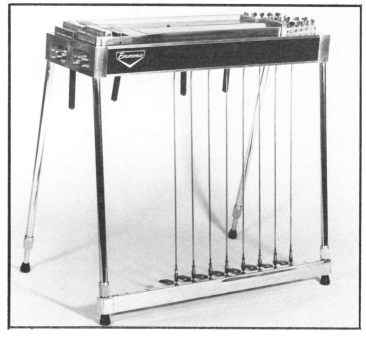

## Pro Model

This guitar comes in both single neck and double neck. The instrument usually has a triple raise and double lower and the necks can vary to 10, 11, 12, 13 and 14 strings with as many as ten pedals and ten knees on the double neck. Some pros even have more! With this capability, the steel guitar has no limits to what it can do. It is already into Hawaiian, Country, Rock, and Jazz. It is truly a challenge for any musician due to its versatility.

# SETTING UP THE PEDAL STEEL

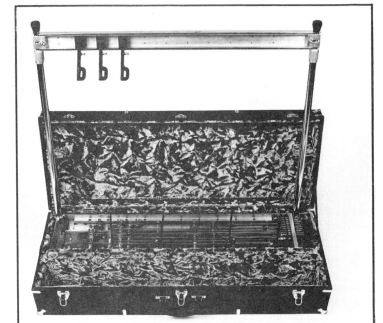

### Two Legs and Pedal Bar

## Step #1

*The steel guitar is set up while the guitar is in the case. Put the two front legs on first—then the pedal bar.*

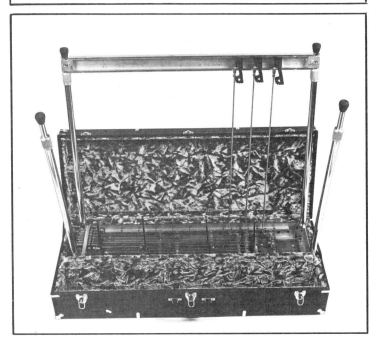

### Steel Set Up In Case

## Step #2

Put the three pedal rods on next. These are numbered 1-2-3 from the right as you are now looking at the steel. Then put the two back legs on. Pull your knee lever into position.

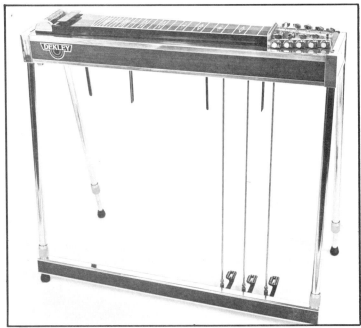

### Steel Guitar in Set Up Position

The steel guitar is disassembled in the case. Reverse the set-up procedure.

# E 9TH CHROMATIC PEDAL TUNING CHART

This tuning is the most accepted one for commercial playing. When the pros were using non-pedal steel guitars, they used the E major, E 7th, A major, A 6th, C# minor, E 13th, and C 6th. The E 9th chromatic tuning is a combination of all of these tunings and has proven successful with the leading pros in Nashville.

# PEDAL STEEL GUITAR TUNING CHART
## E 9th CHROMATIC
### 10 STRINGS • THREE FLOOR PEDALS • FOUR KNEE LEVERS

|     | FLOOR PEDALS USED | | | KNEE LEVERS USED | | | |
|-----|-----|-----|-----|-----|-----|-----|-----|
|     | A   | B   | C   | D   | E   | F   | G   |
| F#  |     |     |     |     |     |     | G   |
| D#  |     |     |     | D   |     |     |     |
| G#  |     | A   |     |     |     |     |     |
| E   |     |     | F#  |     | Eb  | F   |     |
| B   | C#  |     | C#  |     |     |     |     |
| G#  |     | A   |     |     |     |     |     |
| F#  |     |     |     |     |     |     | G   |
| E   |     |     |     |     | Eb  | F   |     |
| D   |     |     |     |     |     |     |     |
| B   | C#  |     |     |     |     |     |     |

7

# TUNING THE PEDAL STEEL GUITAR
## TUNING TO THE PIANO
*Basic Open Tuning*

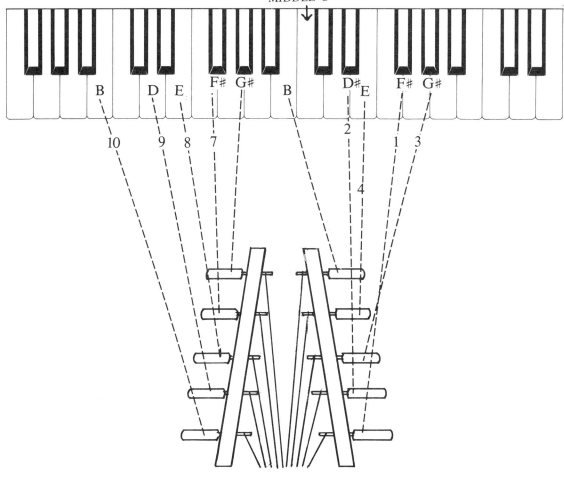

## FLOOR PEDALS AND KNEE LEVERS

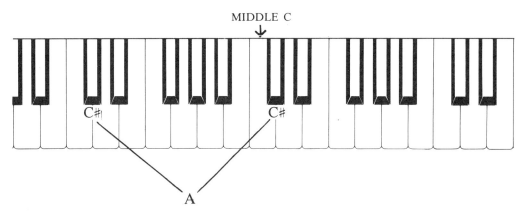

### FLOOR PEDAL

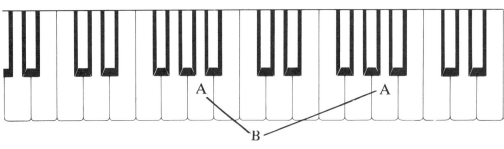

### FLOOR PEDAL

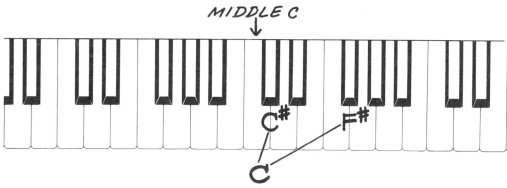

FLOOR PEDAL

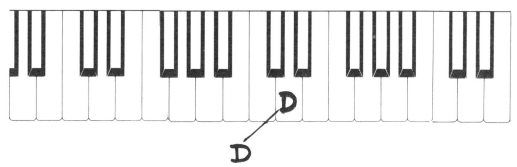

KNEE LEVER (WITH HALF STOP)

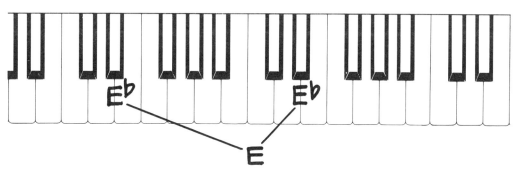

KNEE LEVER

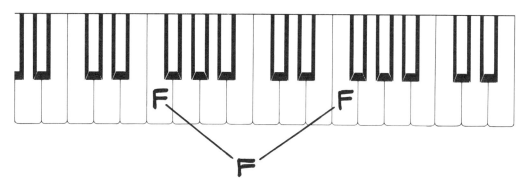

KNEE LEVER

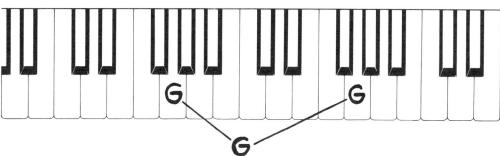

KNEE LEVER

# E 9TH CHROMATIC TUNING GUIDE

You may tune by ear or by the piano. As the steel guitar is a tempered tuning instrument, a lot of the strings are tuned flat to the 440 pitch. Below are settings for the electronic tuning device which will tune your steel as closely as possible.

KORG WT-10

| KORG SETTING | STRING GAUGE | BASIC TUNING | FLOOR PEDALS | | | KNEE PEDALS | | | |
|---|---|---|---|---|---|---|---|---|---|
| | | | A | B | C | D | E | F | G |
| 440 | 013 | F# | | | | | | | G 439.5 |
| 436.5 | 015 | D# | | | | D 439 | | | |
| 436.5 | 011 | G# | | A 438.5 | | | | | |
| 440 | 014 | E | | | F# 437 | | Eb 438 | F 433 | |
| 439.5 | 017 | B | C# 436 | | C# 436 | | | | |
| 436.5 | 020W | G# | | A 438.5 | | | | | |
| 438 | 026W | F# | | | | | | | G 439.5 |
| 440 | 030W | E | | | | | Eb 438 | F 433 | |
| 439 | 034W | D | | | | | | | |
| 439.5 | 036W | B | C# 436 | | | | | | |

Korg WT-12
and Conn Strobe Tuners

| KORG SETTING | STRING GAUGE | BASIC TUNING | FLOOR PEDALS | | | KNEE PEDALS | | | |
|---|---|---|---|---|---|---|---|---|---|
| | | | A | B | C | D | E | F | G |
| O | 013 | F# | | | | | | | G 0 |
| -3.5 | 015 | D# | | | | D-1 | | | |
| -3.5 | 011 | G# | | A-1.5 | | | | | |
| O | 014 | E | | | F#-3 | | Eb-2 | F-7 | |
| -5 | 017 | B | C#-4 | | C#-4 | | | | |
| -3.5 | 020W | G# | | A-1.5 | | | | | |
| -2 | 026W | F# | | | | | | | |
| O | 030W | E | | | | | Eb-2 | F-7 | G 0 |
| -1 | 034W | D | | | | | | | |
| -5 | 036W | B | C#-4 | | | | | | |

*These settings are used with permission from Jeff Newman, Jeffran College, Nashville, TN*

# RIGHT AND LEFT HAND POSITIONS

## Right Hand

Ring and little fingers are extended out with side of palm blocking the strings.

## Right Hand

Ring and little fingers are tucked under with the fingers blocking the treble strings and the palm blocking the bass strings.

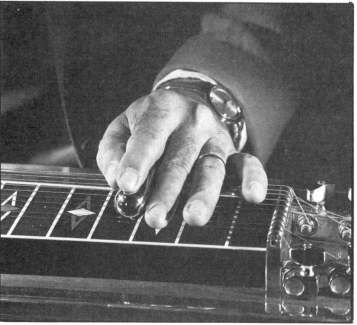

## Left Hand

The ring and little finger rest on the strings.

# TABLATURE INSTRUCTIONS

*(Knowledge of Music Not Required)*

## Strings and Frets

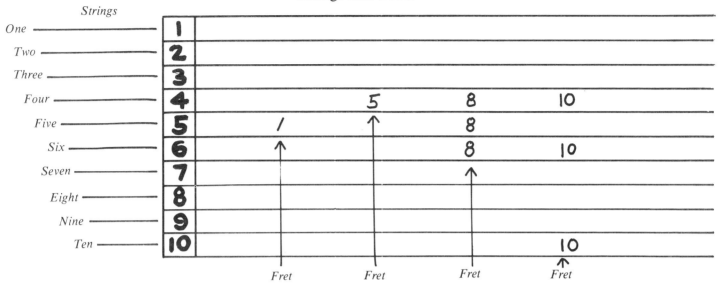

The spaces are numbered downward one thru ten. These are the ten strings of the guitar. The numbers positioned in the spaces are the frets on which you are to place the bar. The three eights (strings 4-5-6) and the three tens (strings 4-6-10) are to be played all three at the same time (chord) using the thumb, first, and second fingers.

# TIMING

## Notes and Diagrams

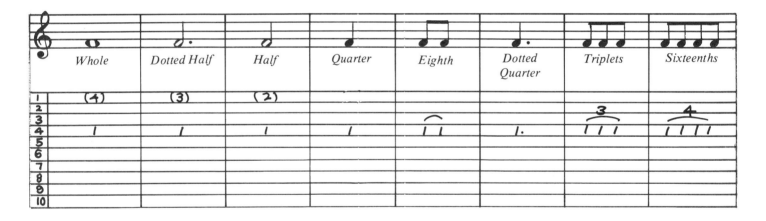

# GLISS OR SLIDES

Gliss = Slide from lower note to the higher note without picking the higher note.

| | |
|---|---|
| 1 | |
| 2 | |
| 3 | |
| 4 | 8 ———— 13 |
| 5 | 8 ———— 13 |
| 6 | 8 ———— 13 |
| 7 | |
| 8 | |
| 9 | |
| 10 | |

Gliss = Slide from the higher note to the lower note without picking the lower note.

| | |
|---|---|
| 1 | |
| 2 | |
| 3 | |
| 4 | 13 ———— 8 |
| 5 | 13 ———— 8 |
| 6 | 13 ———— 8 |
| 7 | |
| 8 | |
| 9 | |
| 10 | |

Gliss Effect With Pedals = Pick the strings without pedals, while the strings are still ringing push the A and B pedals down.

| | |
|---|---|
| 1 | |
| 2 | |
| 3 | |
| 4 | 8 ———— 8 |
| 5 | 8 ———— 8 A |
| 6 | 8 ———— 8 B |
| 7 | |
| 8 | |
| 9 | |
| 10 | |

Gliss Effect With Pedals = Pick the strings with the A and B pedals down. While the strings are still ringing release the A and B pedals.

| | |
|---|---|
| 1 | |
| 2 | |
| 3 | |
| 4 | 8 ———— 8 |
| 5 | 8A ———— 8 |
| 6 | 8B ———— 8 |
| 7 | |
| 8 | |
| 9 | |
| 10 | |

# Finger And Timing Exercise

**Four counts per measure**

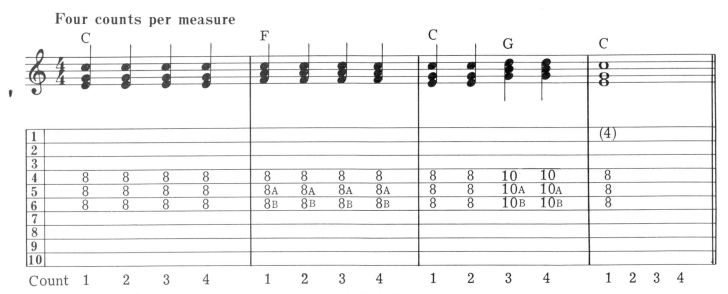

| | | Count 1 | 2 | 3 | 4 | 1 | 2 | 3 | 4 | 1 | 2 | 3 | 4 | 1 | 2 | 3 | 4 |
|---|---|---|---|---|---|---|---|---|---|---|---|---|---|---|---|---|---|
| 1 | | | | | | | | | | | | | | (4) | | | |
| 4 | | 8 | 8 | 8 | 8 | 8 | 8 | 8 | 8 | 8 | 8 | 10 | 10 | 8 | | | |
| 5 | | 8 | 8 | 8 | 8 | 8A | 8A | 8A | 8A | 8 | 8 | 10A | 10A | 8 | | | |
| 6 | | 8 | 8 | 8 | 8 | 8B | 8B | 8B | 8B | 8 | 8 | 10B | 10B | 8 | | | |

Measure #1= No pedals are used for counts 1-2-3-4
Measure #2= A & B pedals are used for counts 1-2-3-4
Measure #3= No pedals for counts 1 & 2
                     A & B pedals for counts 3 & 4
Measure #4= No pedals are used for four counts

**Three counts per measure**

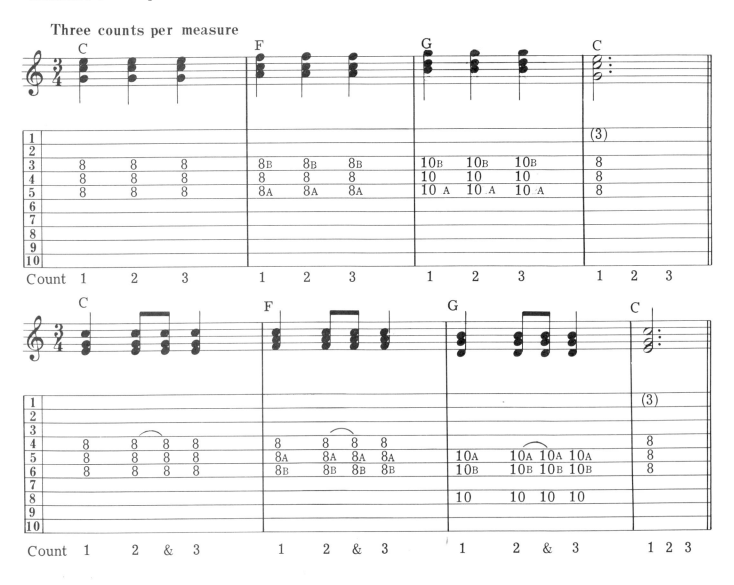

| | | Count 1 | 2 | 3 | 1 | 2 | 3 | 1 | 2 | 3 | 1 | 2 | 3 |
|---|---|---|---|---|---|---|---|---|---|---|---|---|---|
| 1 | | | | | | | | | | | (3) | | |
| 3 | | 8 | 8 | 8 | 8B | 8B | 8B | 10B | 10B | 10B | 8 | | |
| 4 | | 8 | 8 | 8 | 8 | 8 | 8 | 10 | 10 | 10 | 8 | | |
| 5 | | 8 | 8 | 8 | 8A | 8A | 8A | 10 A | 10 A | 10 A | 8 | | |

| | | Count 1 | 2 | & | 3 | 1 | 2 | & | 3 | 1 | 2 | & | 3 | 1 | 2 | 3 |
|---|---|---|---|---|---|---|---|---|---|---|---|---|---|---|---|---|
| 1 | | | | | | | | | | | | | | (3) | | |
| 4 | | 8 | 8 | 8 | 8 | 8 | 8 | 8 | 8 | | | | | 8 | | |
| 5 | | 8 | 8 | 8 | 8 | 8A | 8A | 8A | 8A | 10A | 10A | 10A | 10A | 8 | | |
| 6 | | 8 | 8 | 8 | 8 | 8B | 8B | 8B | 8B | 10B | 10B | 10B | 10B | 8 | | |
| 8 | | | | | | | | | | 10 | 10 | 10 | 10 | | | |

# Warm Up Exercises

Courtesy of Buddy Emmons

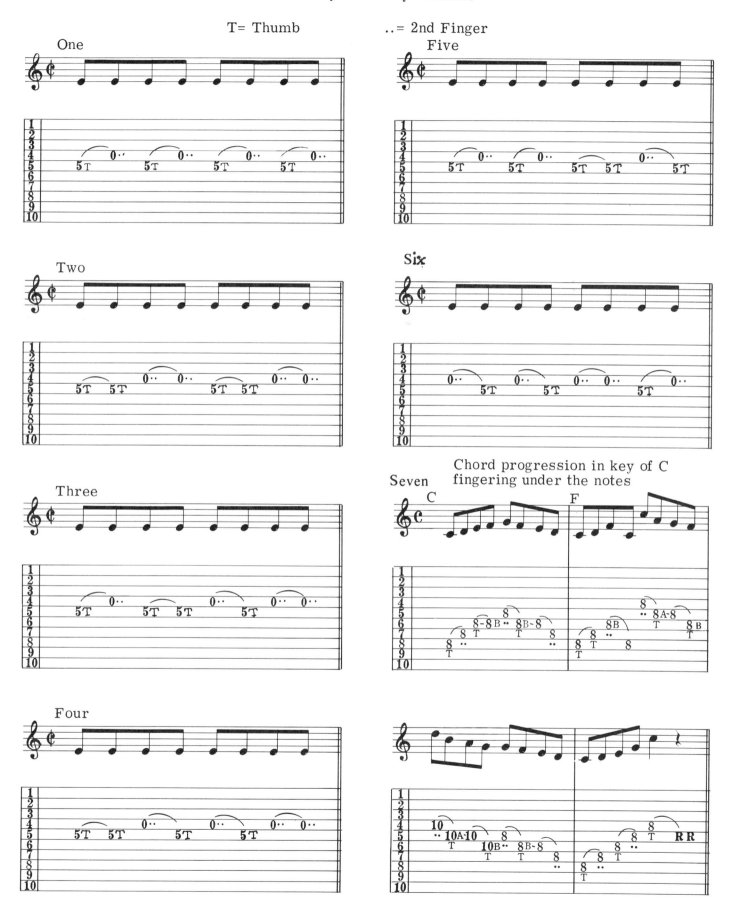

# C Major Scale

Three different approaches to the C scale

Courtesy of Buddy Emmons

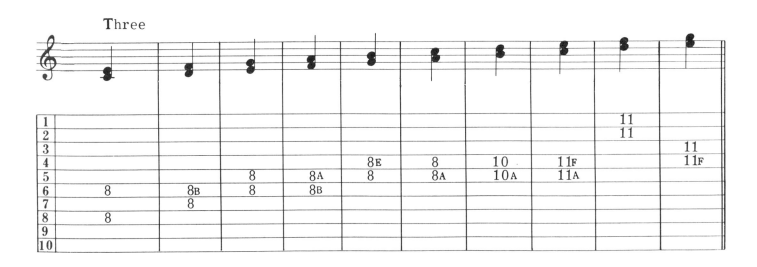

# Blocking Exercises

# Twinkle Steel

## Two And Three Part Harmony

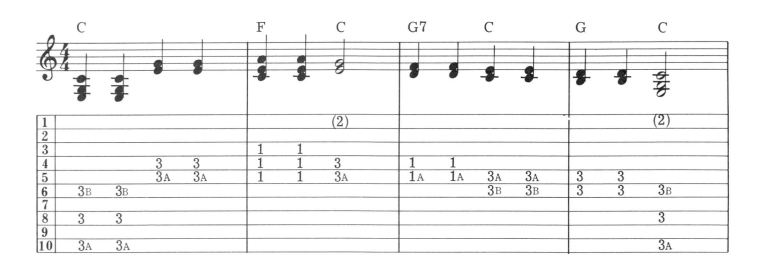

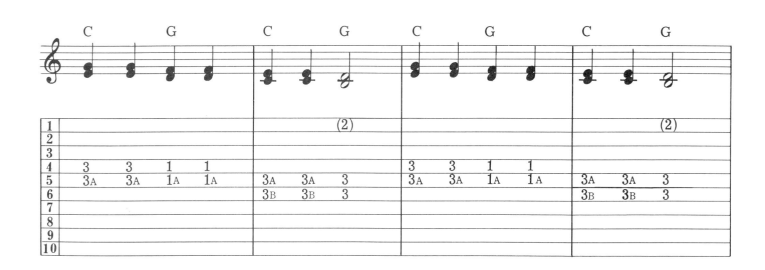

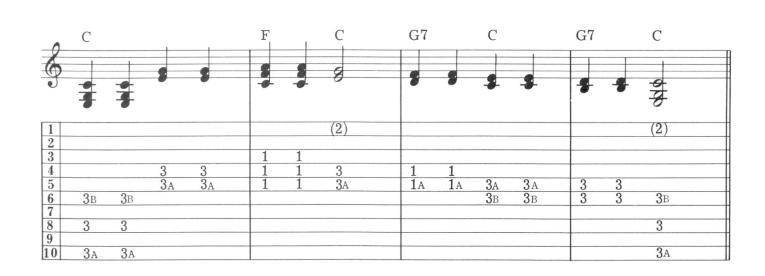

# Twinkle Steel

## Two And Three Part Harmony With Single Note Passages

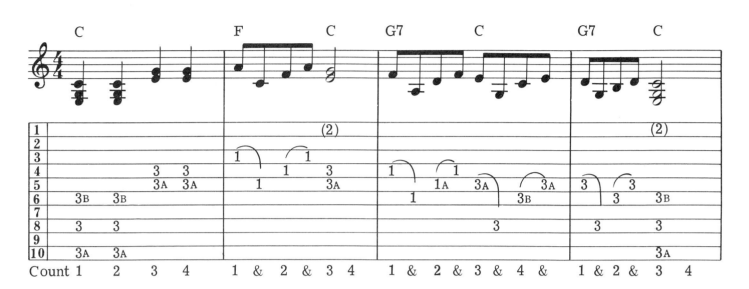

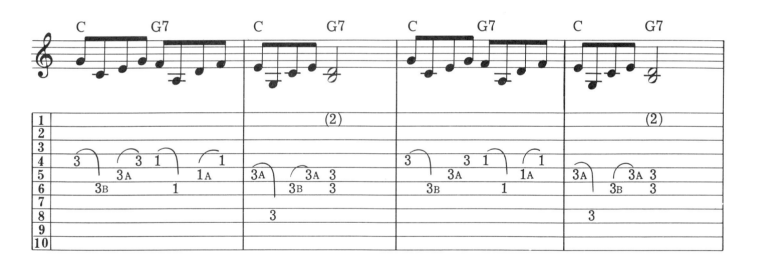

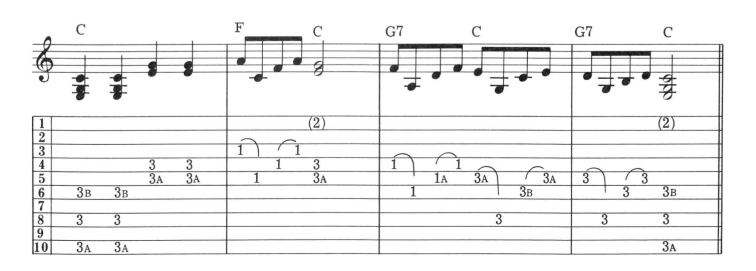

19

**Don Helms**

We are using the chord
pattern 1——5. C ——G

# Go Tell Aunt Rhody
## (The Old Grey Goose Is Dead)

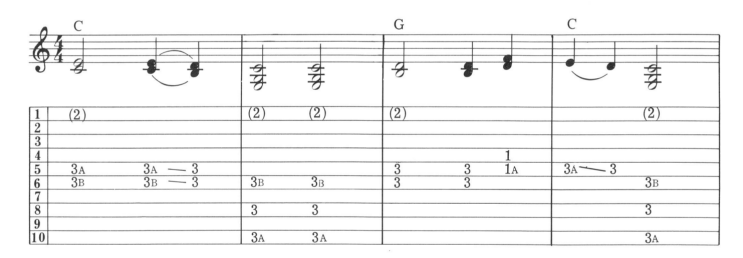

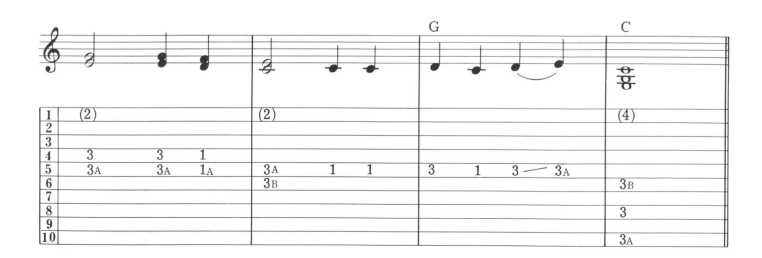

We will now change the chord
pattern to 1 —5⁷. G —G7

C chord

| | |
|---|---|
| 1 | |
| 2 | |
| 3 | |
| 4 | |
| 5 | |
| 6 | 3B |
| 7 | |
| 8 | 3 |
| 9 | |
| 10 | 3A |

G7 chord

| | |
|---|---|
| 1 | |
| 2 | |
| 3 | |
| 4 | 3 |
| 5 | |
| 6 | 3 |
| 7 | |
| 8 | |
| 9 | 3 |
| 10 | |

**Ron Elliot**

# Go Tell Aunt Rhody
### With the 1—5⁷ Chord

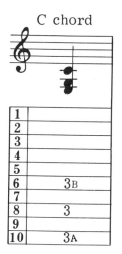
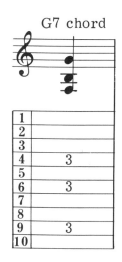

| | C | | | G7 | | | C | | C | |
|---|---|---|---|---|---|---|---|---|---|---|
| 1 | (2) | | (2) | (2) | (2) | | | | (2) | |
| 2 | | | | | | | | | | |
| 3 | | | | | | | | | | |
| 4 | | | | | | | | 1 | | |
| 5 | 3A | 3A — 3 | | | | 3 | 3 | 1A | 3A — 3 | |
| 6 | 3B | 3B — 3 | | 3B | 3B | 3 | 3 | 1 | 3 — 3 | 3B |
| 7 | | | | | | | | | | |
| 8 | | | | 3 | 3 | | | | | 3 |
| 9 | | | | | | 3 | | | 3 — 3 | |
| 10 | | | | 3A | 3A | | | | | 3A |

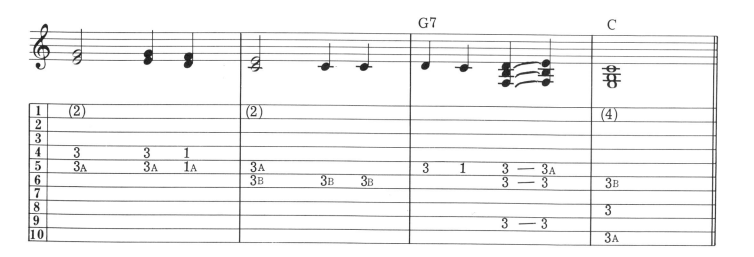

21

**Mike Smith**

Some tunes can be
played in their entirety
on one fret with the
use of the pedals.

Chord changes
G  Tonic
C  Subdominant
D7 Dominant seventh

# Goodnight Ladies

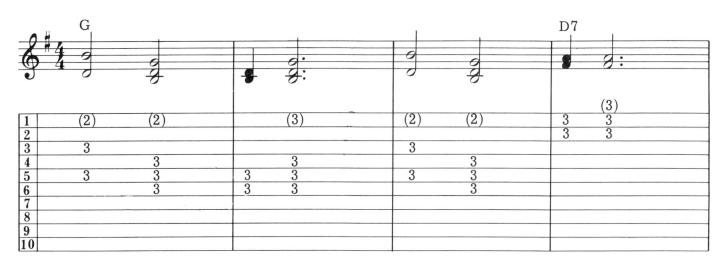

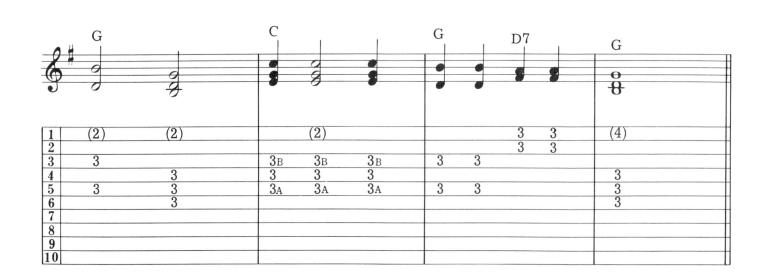

**Little Roy Wiggins**

The tune "Skip to My Lou" is an old folk tune that is adaptable to the steel guitar.

Chord changes
 C tonic
 G7 dominant seventh

# Skip To My Lou

Key of C
**Moderato**

Traditional

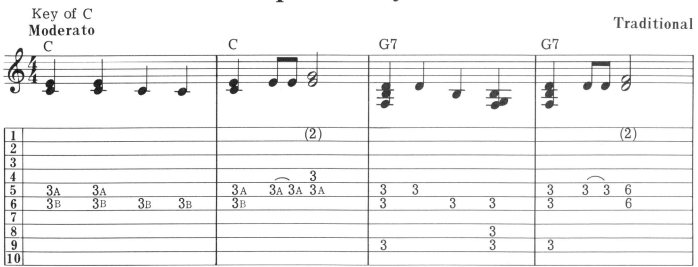

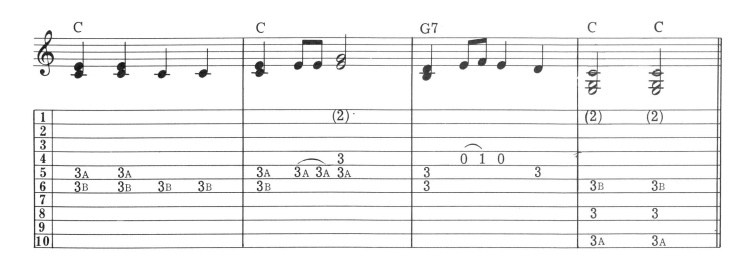

# Single Note Picking

Here is the finger pattern for this single string run.

- T = Thumb
- ˙ = First finger
- ˙˙ = Second finger
- ♪ = Grace note. It's played quickly and receives no count.

Run ♯ Two

Watch out for this one!
The second finger plays the fourth string, the thumb plays all the other notes,

**Run #1**

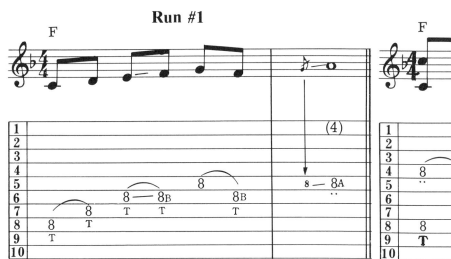

**Run #2**

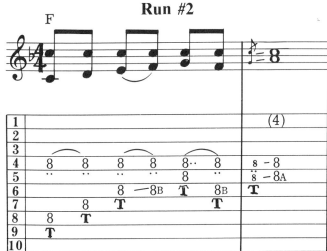

**Run #3**

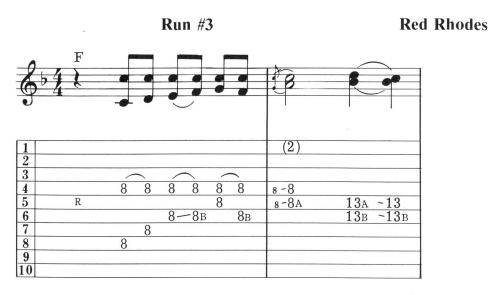

**Red Rhodes**

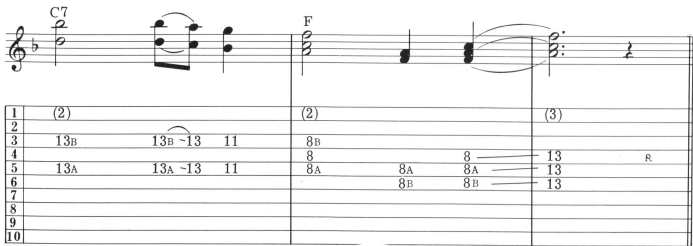

24

# Fast Finger Exercise

*Exercise*

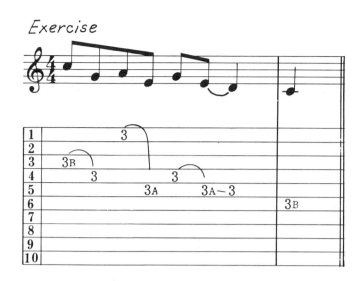

Right hand blocking is very important here. Whatever method of blocking you are using, you must be good at it. Remember—Do not block by picking the bar off the strings, block with the right hand.

# Green Country

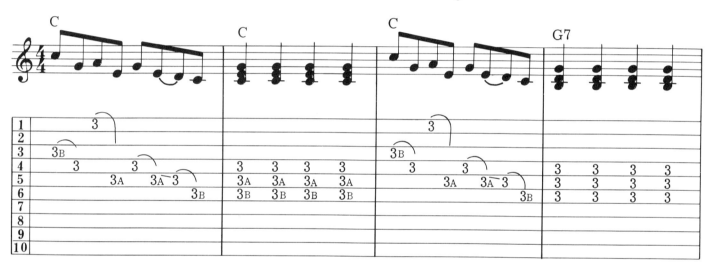

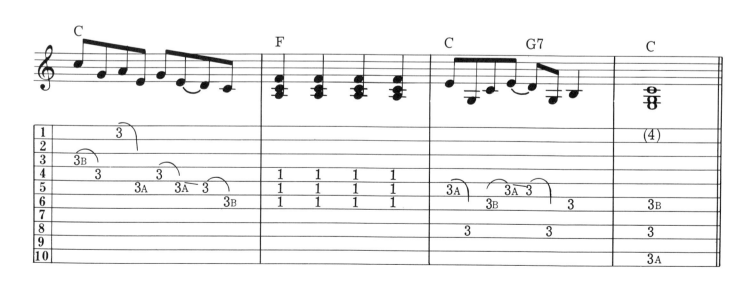

**Hal Rugg**

# Use Of The Third Pedal

C Chord

| 1 | |
|---|---|
| 2 | |
| 3 | |
| 4 | 8 |
| 5 | 8 |
| 6 | 8 |
| 7 | |
| 8 | |
| 9 | |
| 10 | |

D minor Chord

| 1 | |
|---|---|
| 2 | |
| 3 | |
| 4 | 8c |
| 5 | 8c |
| 6 | 8b |
| 7 | |
| 8 | |
| 9 | |
| 10 | |

B. It can be used as a substitute for the dominant seventh. The above example is in the key of C. The dominant seventh in the key of C is G7. So, the B and C pedal used at the eighth fret can be substituted for the G7 chord. Here is a rule to follow that will explain why you can use this combination (D minor) as a substitute for the G7 chord.

Rule: When the dominant seventh chord appears, take the 5th of that chord and make it a minor 7th. Go one more step and construct the G9 chord.

## Example

G9 chord
G B D F A
1-3-5-7-9

D minor 7th
D F A C

The notes D F A
are in both chords.

26

**Alvino Rey**

# B And C Pedals G7 To C

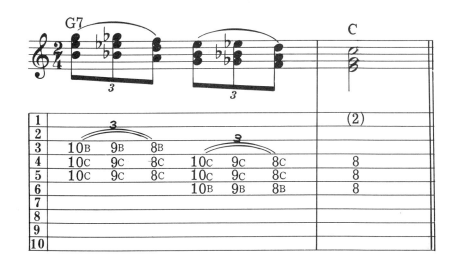

| | | | | | | | C |
|---|---|---|---|---|---|---|---|
| **1** | | | | | | | (2) |
| **2** | | | | | | | |
| **3** | 10B | 9B | 8B | | | | |
| **4** | 10C | 9C | 8C | 10C | 9C | 8C | 8 |
| **5** | 10C | 9C | 8C | 10C | 9C | 8C | 8 |
| **6** | | | | 10B | 9B | 8B | 8 |
| **7** | | | | | | | |
| **8** | | | | | | | |
| **9** | | | | | | | |
| **10** | | | | | | | |

**The Chords**

CHORDS
G7 to C

"Technical terms"
"Dominant 7th to tonic"

"Number method"
5 to 1

# The Bee Cee Swing

Dewitt Scott

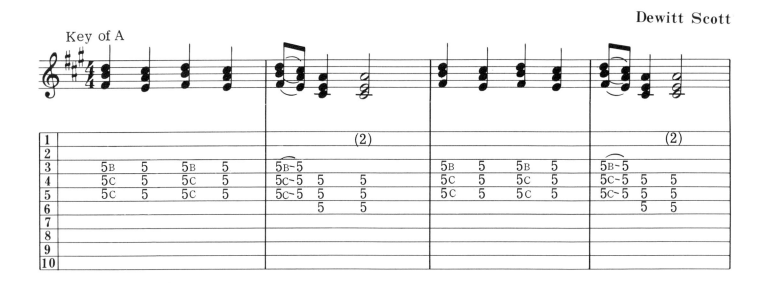

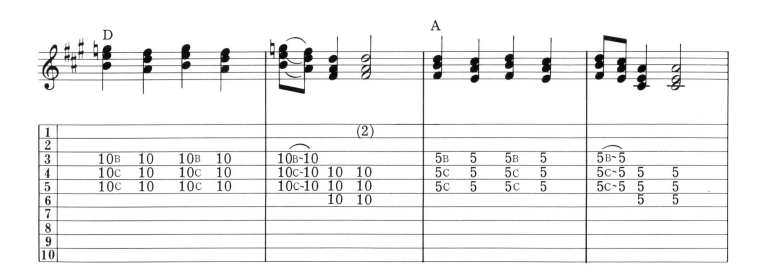

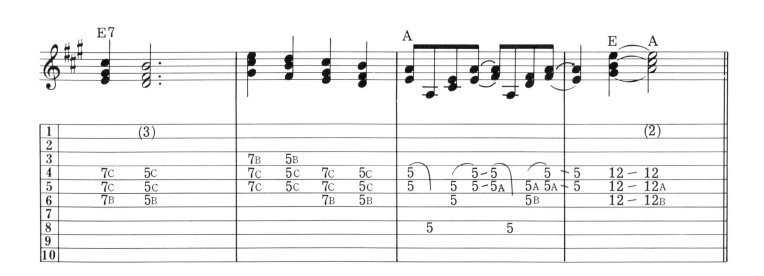

# Intro Mixing The A-B And C Pedals

## Intro In 4/4 Time

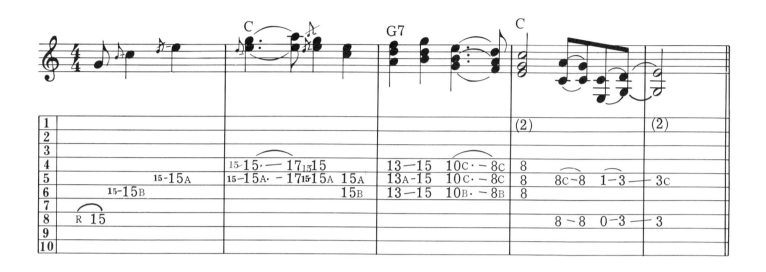

## Intro In 3/4 Time

Note: Any similarity between these intros and the ones you may have heard on hit records is purely intentional!

Here is a tricky way of playing an exercise in a waltz beat. The exercise will be in three parts, then the run will be used in the song "Mississippi Waltz". The first run is played with the second finger only.

The second run is played with the thumb. When you can play run #1 and run #2 with ease, then try run #3. It combines both runs together and you will find that it is a little more difficult.

### Run ♯ One

| String | | | | |
|---|---|---|---|---|
| 1 | | | | (2) |
| 2 | | 3 .. | 2 .. | |
| 3 | | | | |
| 4 | 3 | | | R |
| 5 | .. | | | 3A .. |
| 6 | | | | |
| 7 | | | | |
| 8 | | | | |
| 9 | | | | |
| 10 | | | | |

### Run ♯ Two

| String | | | | |
|---|---|---|---|---|
| 1 | | | | (2) |
| 2 | | | | |
| 3 | | | | |
| 4 | | | | R |
| 5 | | | | |
| 6 | | | 2B | 3B |
| 7 | | 3 | T | T |
| 8 | 3 | T | | |
| 9 | T | | | |
| 10 | | | | |

### Run ♯ Three

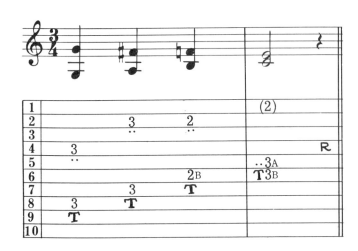

30

# Mississippi Waltz

Using the thumb and second finger exercise
and the E knee lever.

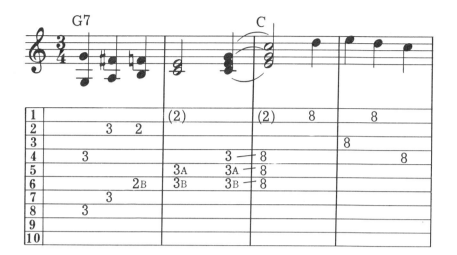

**Norm Hamlett**

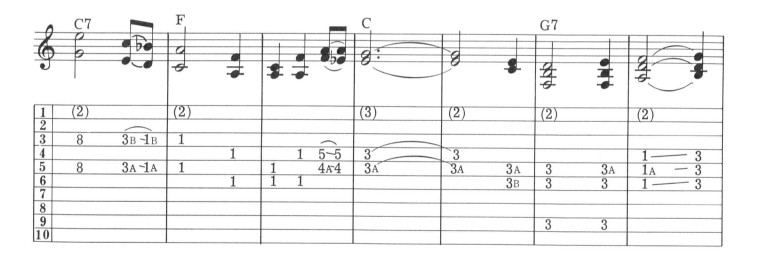

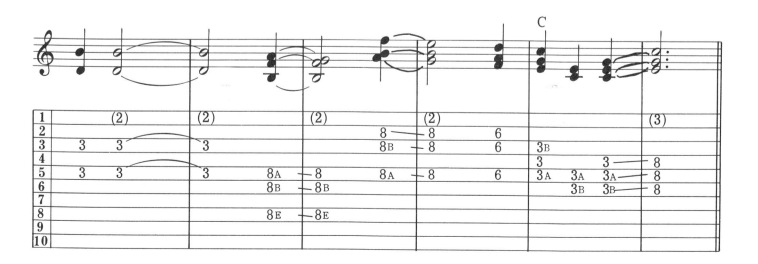

# The Old "F" Knee Lever

The "F" knee lever opens up a whole new position for you. It can be used as a seventh or ninth chord, and with the "A" pedal it becomes a major chord. The "F" knee lever raises the two E strings four and eight to F.

| String | G Chord | G | G7 | G | G | G7 | G | G7 |
|---|---|---|---|---|---|---|---|---|
| 1 | | | | | | | | |
| 2 | | | | | | | | |
| 3 | | | | 3 | | | 6 | 6 |
| 4 | 3 | | | 3 | 6F | 6F | 6F | 6F |
| 5 | 3 | 6A | 6 | 3 | 6A | 6 | 6A | 6 |
| 6 | 3 | 6 | 6 | | 6 | 6 | | |
| 7 | | | | | | | | |
| 8 | | 6F | 6F | | | | | |
| 9 | | | | | | | | |
| 10 | | | | | | | | |

These combinations are used quite frequently by the Nashville recording steel players.   Here is a simple run that has been used over and over.

**Neil Flanz**

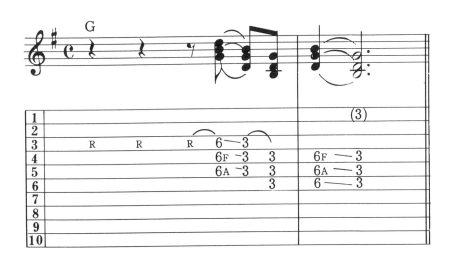

**Bob White**

# The "D" Knee Lever

When you play a 1950's rock tune this knee lever can be a valuable thing to have. It lowers the second string one half tone and becomes the seventh chord. The G position at the third fret would become G7 by using this "D" knee lever. Here is a good old rock and roll lick.

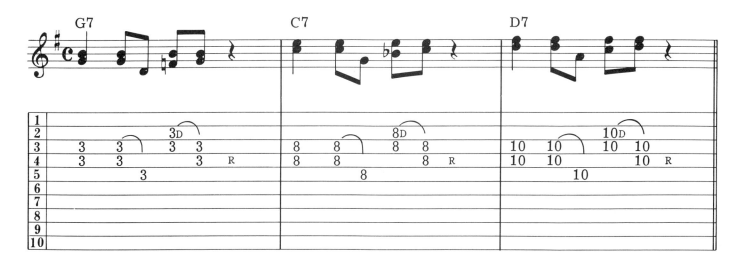

33

**Lynn Owsley**

**Leon McAuliffe**

**Bobby Caldwell** –The Steel Players Friend.

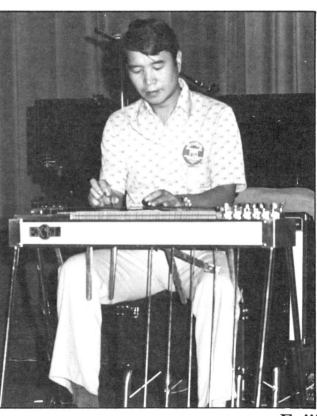

**Mitsou Fujii**
*Japan*

# The Doodle Bug Rock

Note-leave your D knee lever down for the first 8 measures.

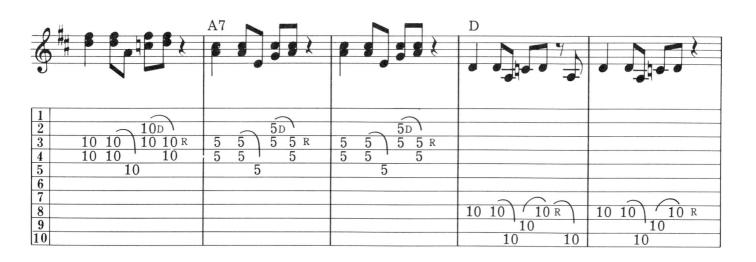

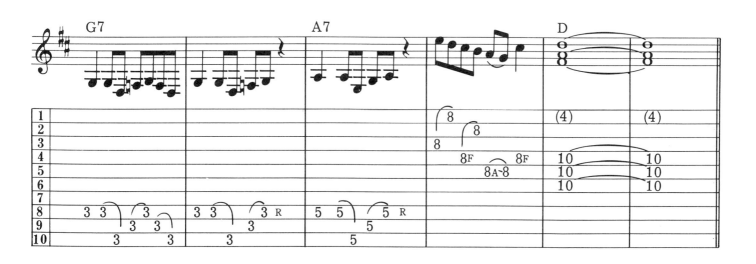

**Koos Biel**
*–Holland*

## Doodle Bug Runs

The tune Doodle Bug Rock is made up of runs that can be used in most 1950's rock tunes. The more runs you know, the more variety you can put into a tune.

Here are two more runs that will work quite well. Perfect the runs, then try the Doodle Bug Rock with these new runs.

Run # One                    Run # Two

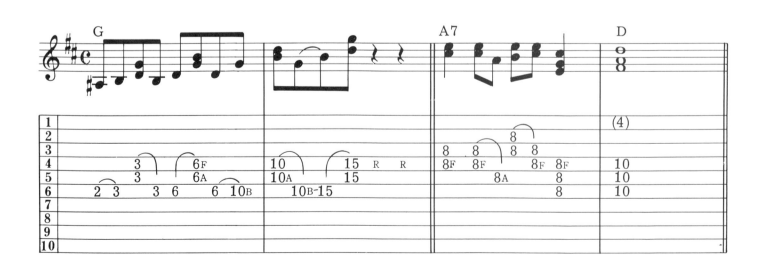

36

# The Doodle Bug Rock

## With The New Runs

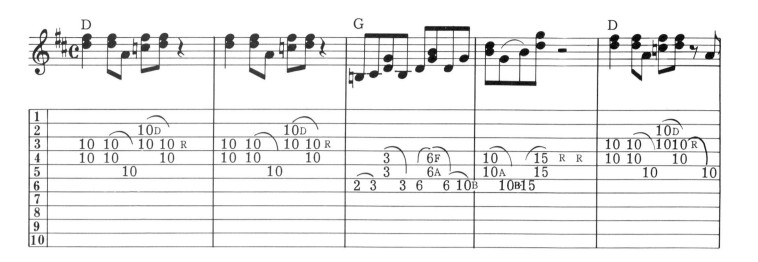

37

# The G Knee Lever

Raise Strings 1 And 7

# More About Blocking

## Augmented Chord

With the bar at the eighth fret, playing strings 5-1-2 the chord is G. With the G knee lever the chord is G augmented.

### Example

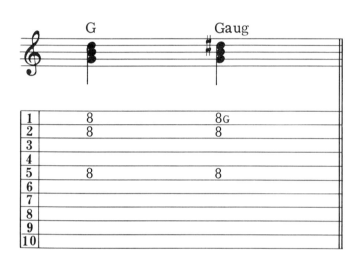

The augmented chord is used as a passing chord.

### Example

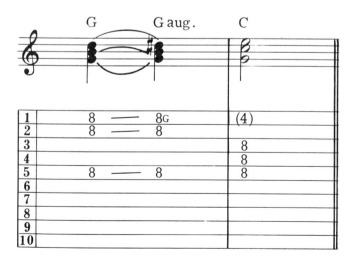

## Very Fast Picking

The right hand rests on the strings just in front of the pickups. What you are doing is permanently blocking the strings-It won't be a true note, but you won't have to keep raising and lowering the right hand as in the normal way.

The fingers and thumb of the left hand can be a big help in blocking.

# More About The G Knee Lever

### It's A Seventh Chord

Below are the C7, F7, and G7 chord locations using the A & B pedals, plus the G knee lever.

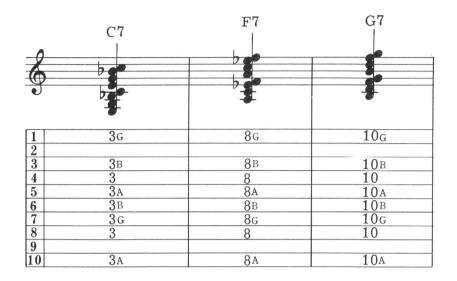

| | C7 | F7 | G7 |
|---|---|---|---|
| 1 | 3G | 8G | 10G |
| 2 | | | |
| 3 | 3B | 8B | 10B |
| 4 | 3 | 8 | 10 |
| 5 | 3A | 8A | 10A |
| 6 | 3B | 8B | 10B |
| 7 | 3G | 8G | 10G |
| 8 | 3 | 8 | 10 |
| 9 | | | |
| 10 | 3A | 8A | 10A |

**Bud Isaacs**

## Example ♯ One

C chord to C7

| | C | | | C7 |
|---|---|---|---|---|
| 1 | | | | 4 |
| 2 | | | | |
| 3 | | | | |
| 4 | 3 | 2 | 1 | |
| 5 | 3A | 2A | 1A | 3A |
| 6 | | | | 3B |
| 7 | | | | 3G |
| 8 | | | | |
| 9 | | | | |
| 10 | | | | |

## Example ♯ Two

C7 run - up tempo

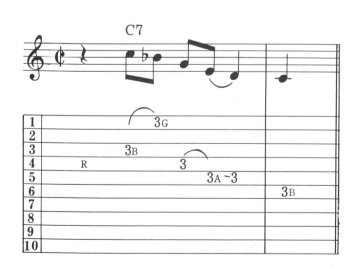

| | | | |
|---|---|---|---|
| 1 | | 3G | |
| 2 | | | |
| 3 | 3B | | |
| 4 | R | 3 | |
| 5 | | 3A ~3 | |
| 6 | | | 3B |
| 7 | | | |
| 8 | | | |
| 9 | | | |
| 10 | | | |

# Red River Valley
## Pedals And Knee Pedals

A B C floor pedals        E and F knee levers

$A\frac{1}{2}$ = Release the A pedal only $\frac{1}{2}$ instead of all the way

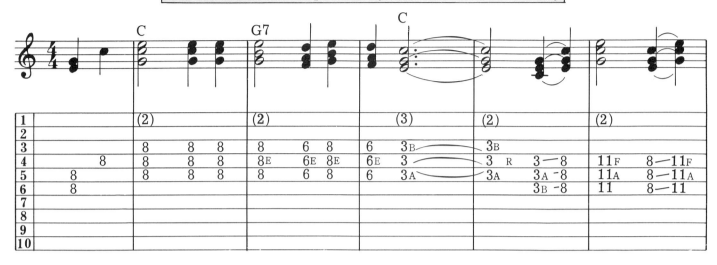

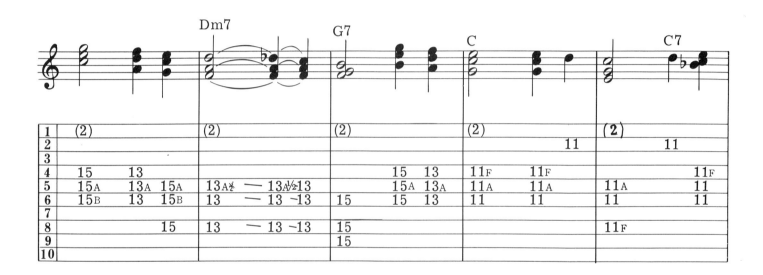

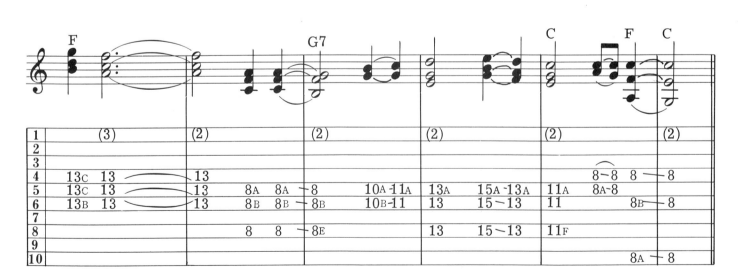

# Runs, Licks And Fills

Do not block-Let all strings sustain

# Aura Lee

Arranged by Dewitt Scott

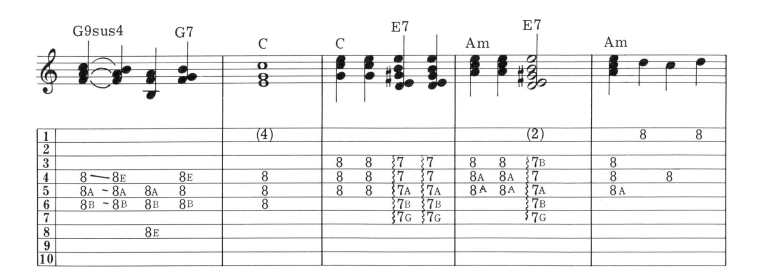

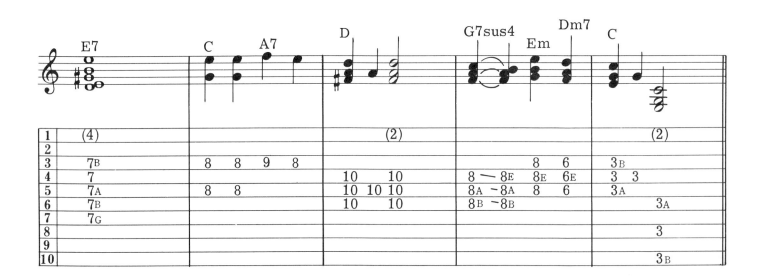

**Pat Heller**

# Moveable Major Scale

## (Ionian Mode)

This major scale will have a complete octave plus three more notes added on.

Do Re Mi Fa Sol La Ti Do Re Me Fa

### E Major Scale Open Position

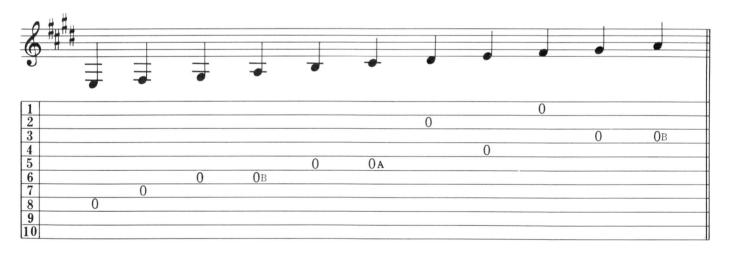

### Some Other Major Scales

Same Strings-Same Pedals

| | |
|---|---|
| 1st fret = F scale | 8th fret = C scale |
| 3rd fret = G scale | 10th fret = D scale |
| 5th fret = A scale | 11th fret = E♭ scale |
| 6th fret = B♭ scale | 12th fret = E scale |

# Playing A Tune On One Fret

## Utilizing The C Scale, 8th Fret

My Bonnie Lies Over the Ocean

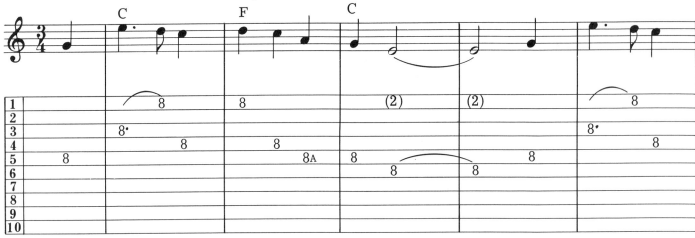

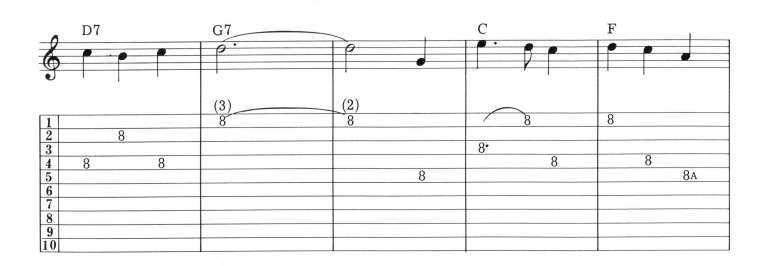

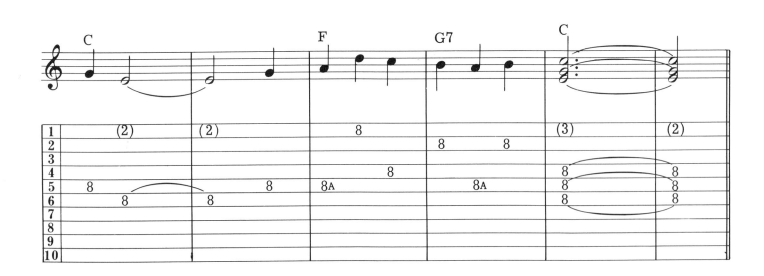

# C Scale Harmonized

Scale number one is written with the root showing three notes with the harmony written below, (3rd and 5th). All other notes of the scale have two notes (in thirds).

## Scale Number One

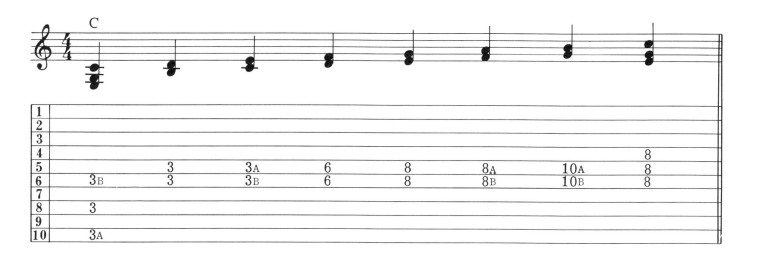

## Scale Number Two

Scale number two is in three note harmony. Scale number one showed the simple way of harmonizing all the notes of the C scale with the C chord as a guide. Scale number two follows the major-minor and diminished rules.

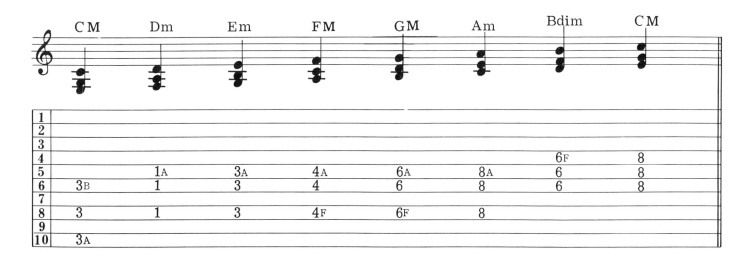

# Old Black Joe

**Moderato**

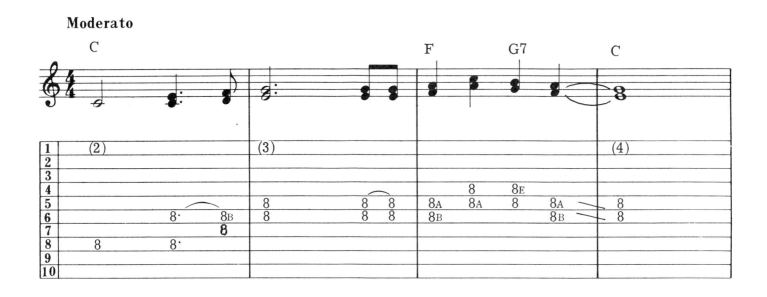

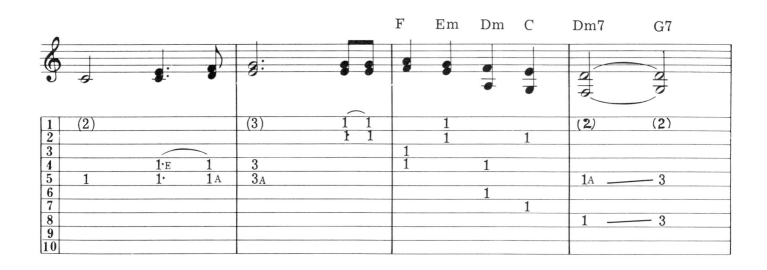

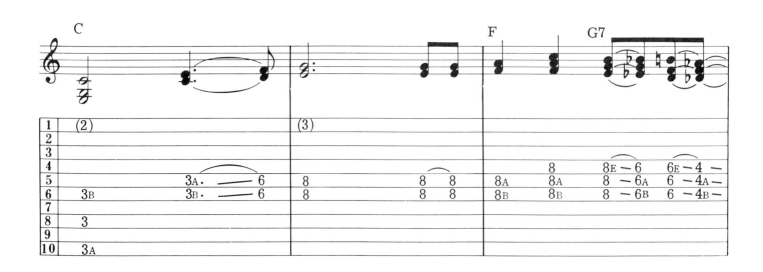

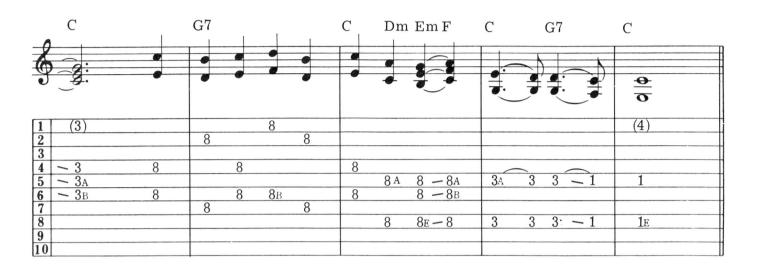

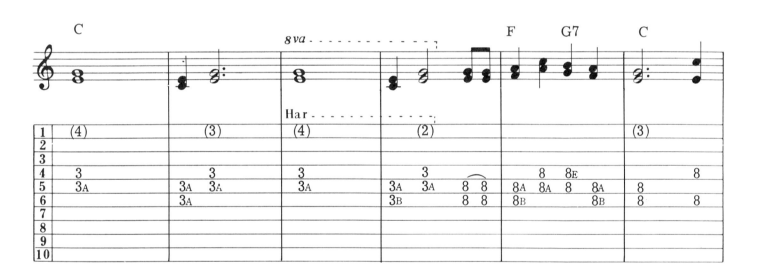

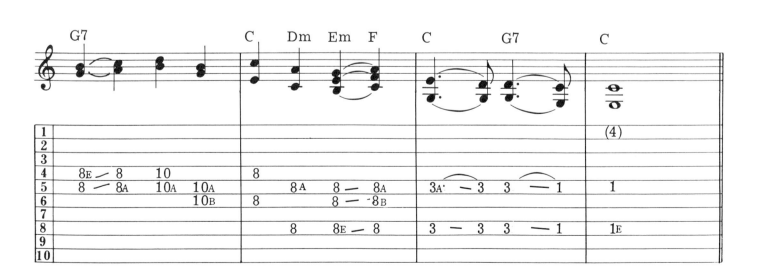

# Silent Night

Here is another song that you can play on one fret. Further along in the book we will play it again using more chords and different positions.

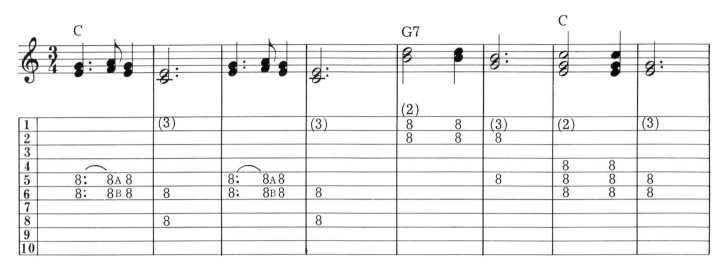

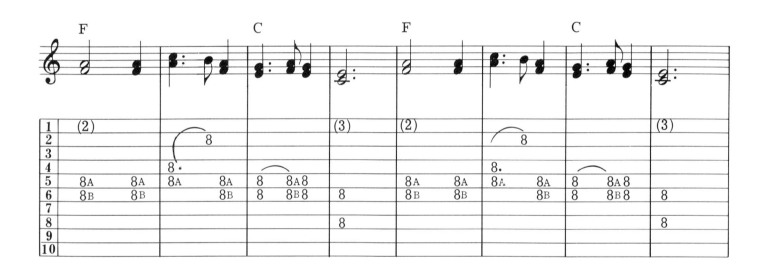

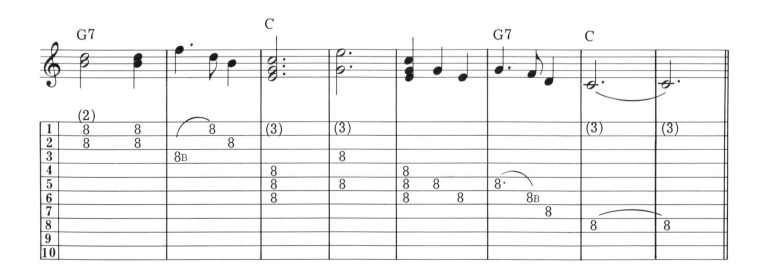

**Glenn Rieuf, Jr.**

**Ernie Hagar**

**George Edwards**

**Kenny Kitching**

*Australia*

# Sounds Of The Dobro

The Dobro was the first guitar used with three finger picks and a steel bar. A metal resonator was installed on the top of the guitar to amplify the sound. One of the most popular songs of its day was the "Great Speckled Bird".

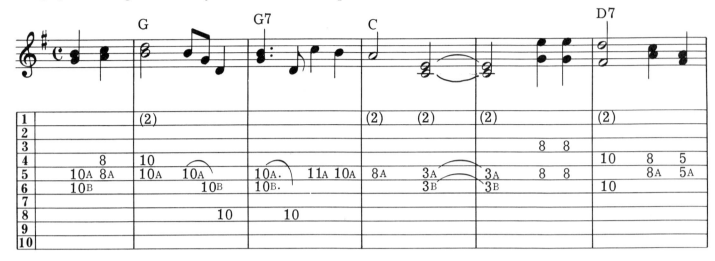

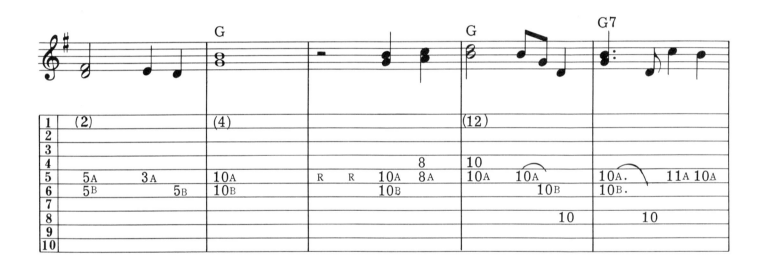

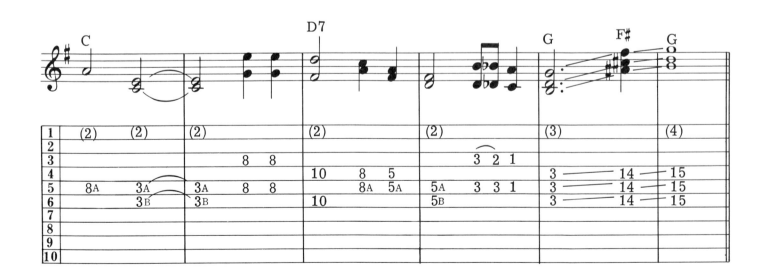

# Dobro Sounds

Dobro quickly became a very important part of Bluegrass groups. Being a nonelectric instrument, it fit right in.

## Bluegrass Runs

① Keep A&B down thru the exercise.

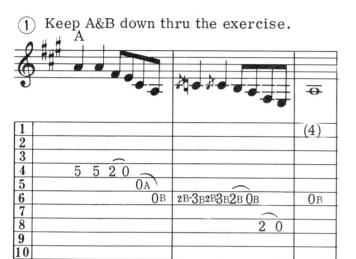

④ x = Don't pick-let the bar play the note.

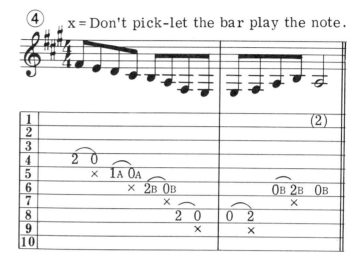

② Banjo run-you'll recognize this right away!

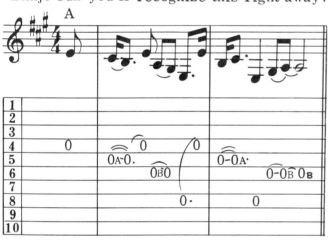

⑤ An "Easy" dobro run-but is used constantly.

③ A typical dobro run

⑥ Another "Easy" run

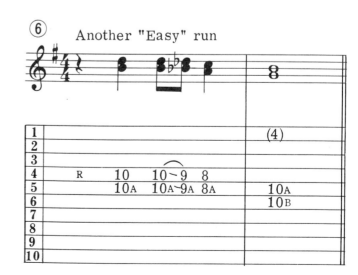

51

# 1950's Rock

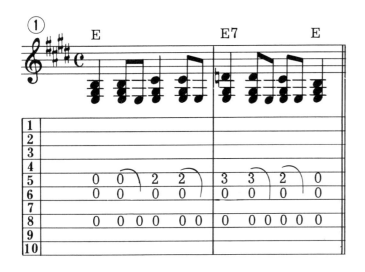

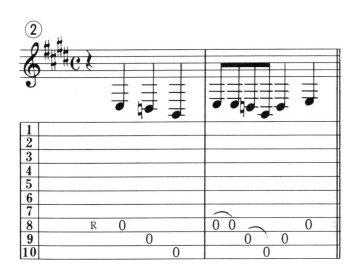

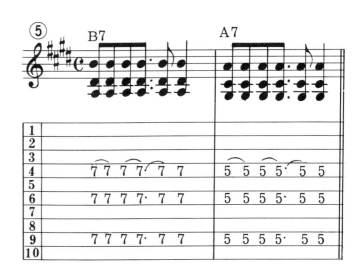

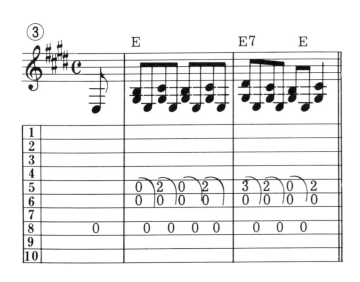

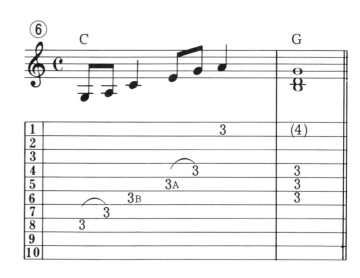

# The Boogie Woogie

Style #1. Play the tune as it appears using Quarter notes.

Style #2. Play the tune in eighth notes-but double up the notes you play! Play two G notes- two B notes-two D notes-two E notes and so on to the last measure- -play the last measure as it is written.

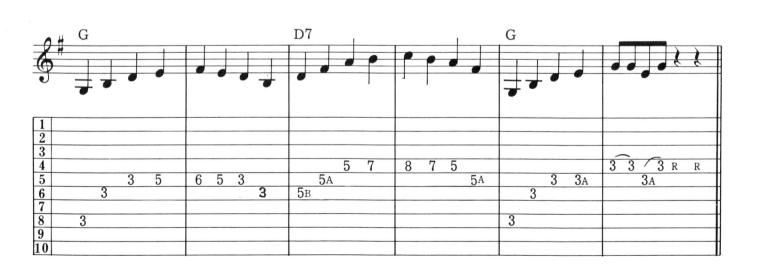

# The "A" Pedal Swing

A continuation of the Boogie Woogie and it is played with the "A" pedal down throughout the tune.

by Dewitt Scott

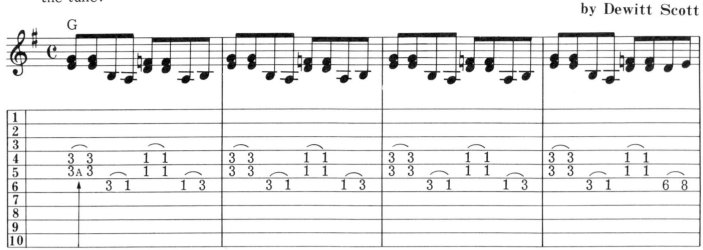

Leave it down throughout the entire song.

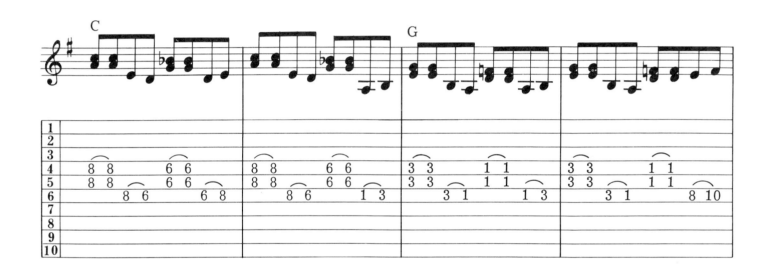

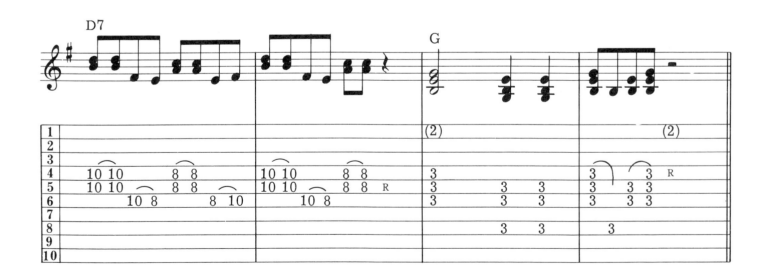

54

# Western Swing Ride

by Dewitt Scott

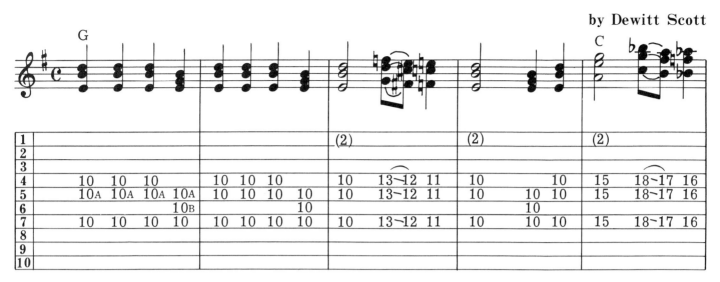

Leave the A and B pedals down throughout the entire song.

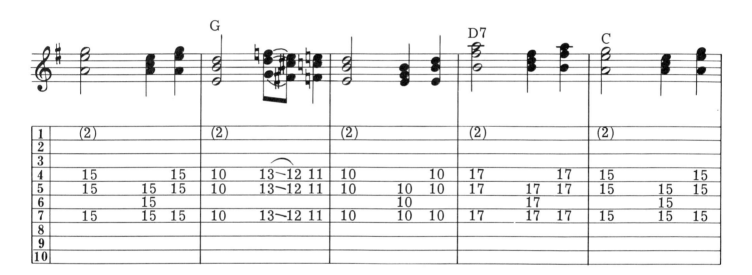

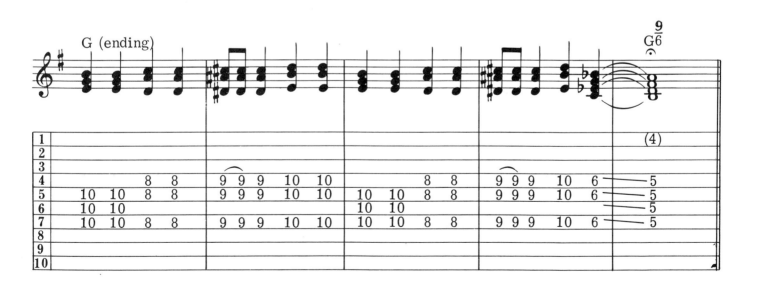

55

# Recognizable Intros

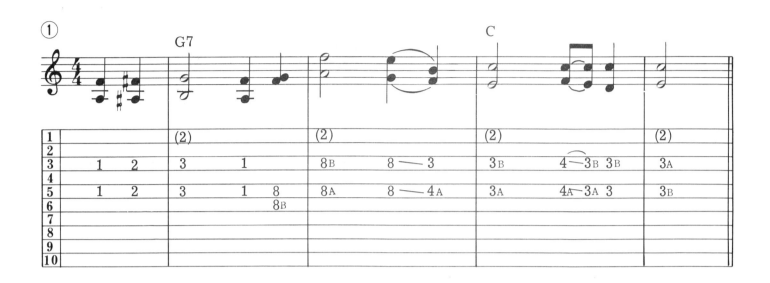

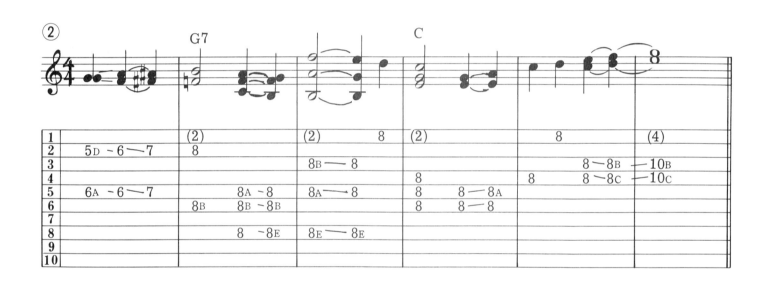

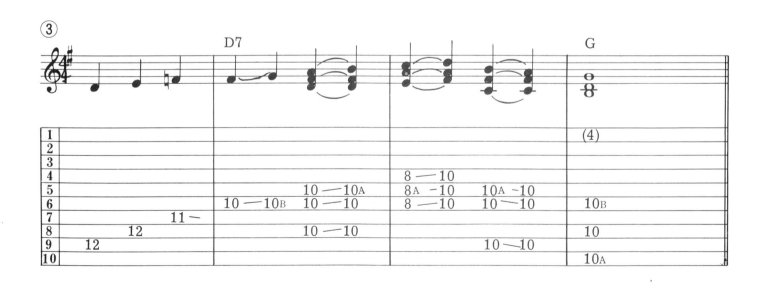

# A Snappy Intro

**Maurice Anderson**

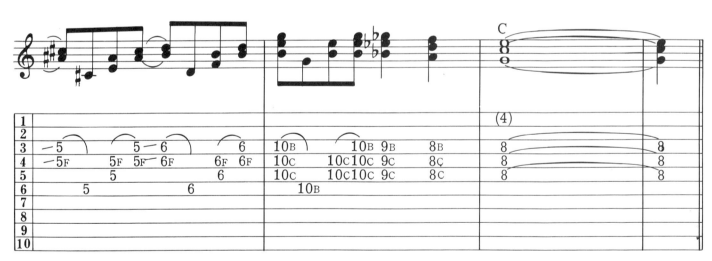

When played with a medium to fast tempo, this intro is very effective. For best results position your left foot over the B and C pedals. This way you will be ready for the third measure.

# The Banjo Roll

**Bob Lucier** *–Canada*

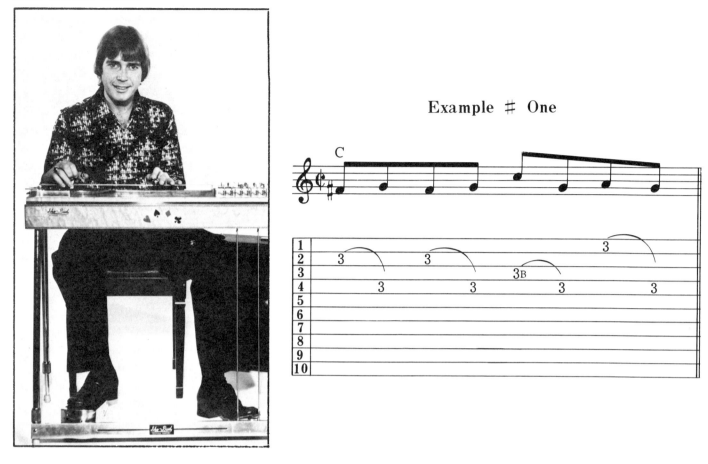

## Example # One

Blocking: Block by resting the edge of the palm of the right hand permanently on the strings, close to the pickup.

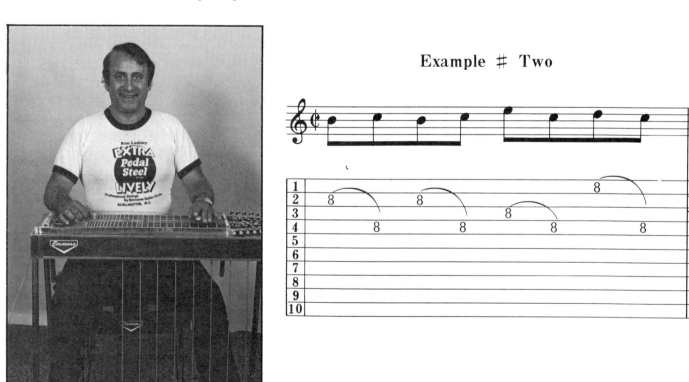

## Example # Two

**George Xanthos** *–Australia*

**Gene O'Neal**

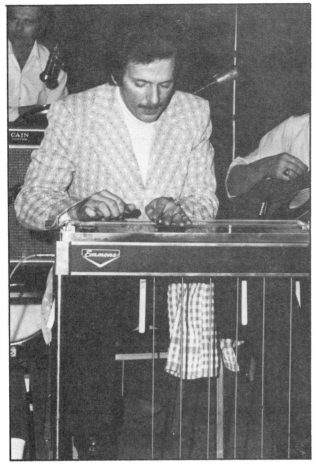

**Sonny Burnette**

**Lloyd Green**

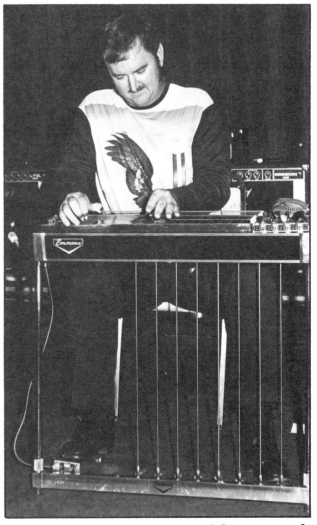

59

**Weldon Myrick**

# My Old Kentucky Home

Arranged by Dewitt Scott

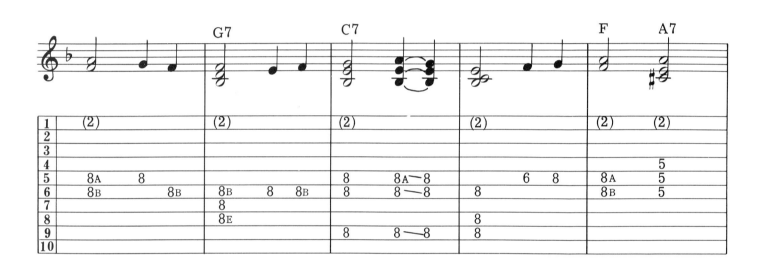

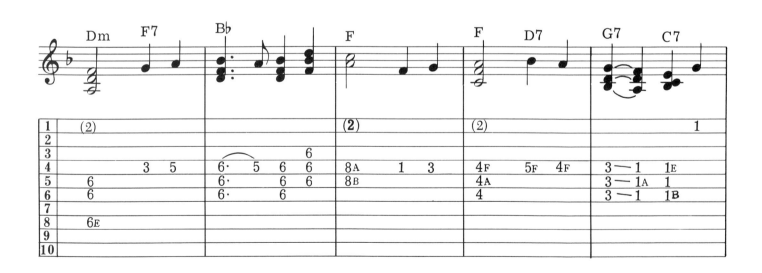

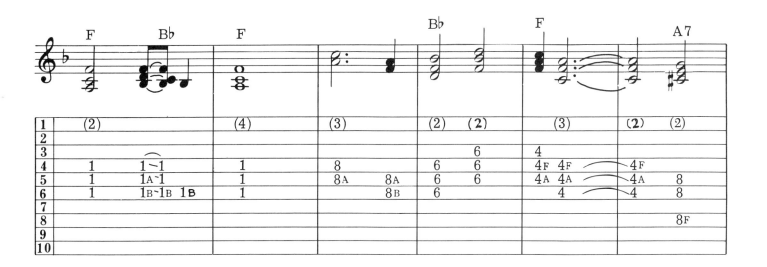

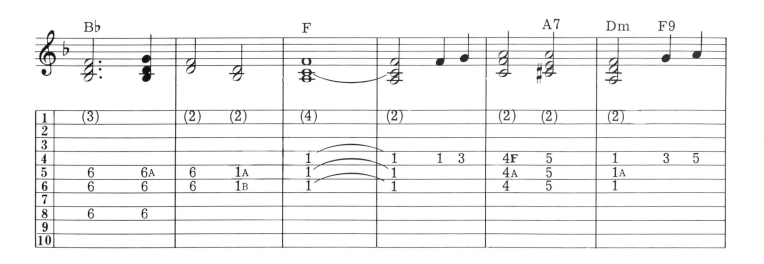

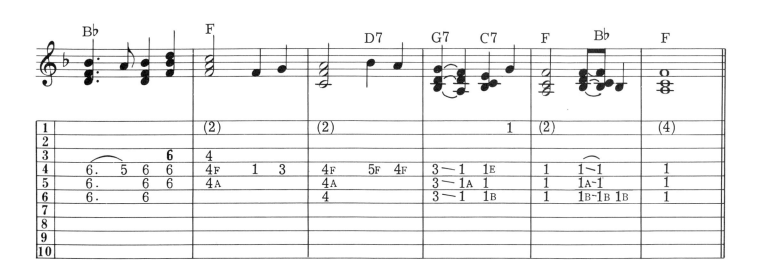

# Silent Night

As we promised earlier in the book, here is Silent Night using more chords, more pedals and different positions.

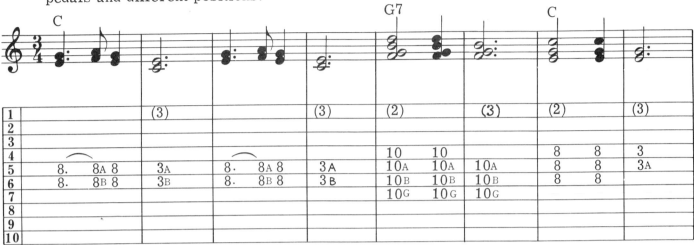

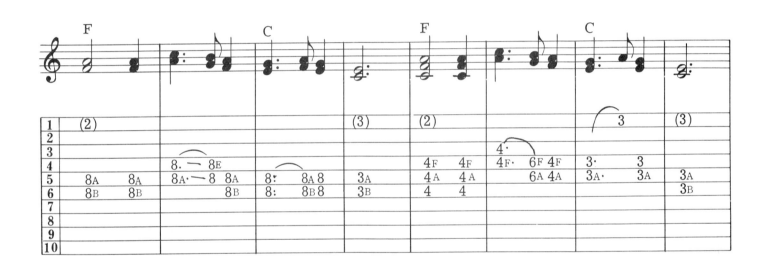

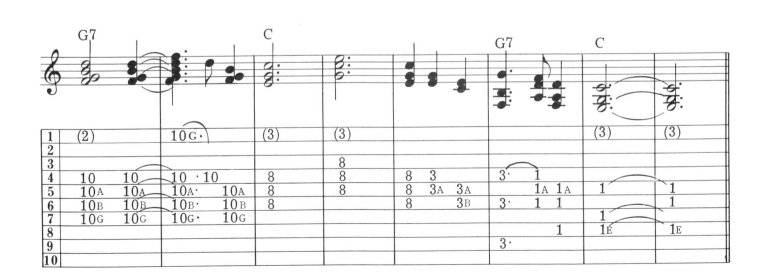

# Marines Hymn

Arranged by Dewitt Scott

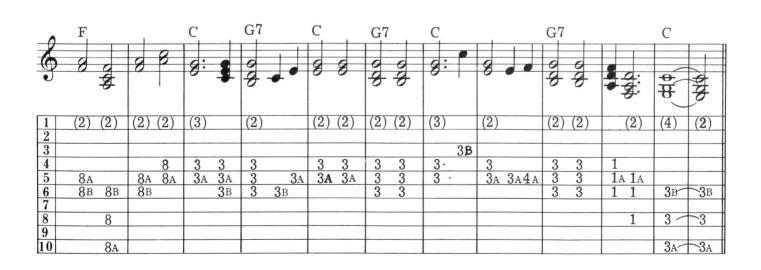

**System 1**

| | C | | G7 | | C | | G7 | | C | | | C | |
|---|---|---|---|---|---|---|---|---|---|---|---|---|---|
| **1** | (2) | (2) | (2) | (2) | (3) | | (2) | | (2) | (2) | (3) | (4) | | (2) | (2) |
| **2** | | | | | | | | | | | | | | |
| **3** | | | | | 3B | | | | | | | | | |
| **4** | 3 | 3 | 3 | 3 | 3 | | 3 | | 3 | 3 | 1 | | | 3 | 3 |
| **5** | 3A | 3A | 3A | 3 | 3 | 3A | | 3A | 3A 4A | 3 | 3 | 1A 1A | | 3A | 3A | 3A |
| **6** | 3B | | | 3 | 3 | | | | | 3 | 3 | 1 1 | 3B ⌒ 3B | 3B |
| **7** | | | | | | | | | | | | | | |
| **8** | | | | | | | | | | | 1 | 3 ⌒ 3 | |
| **9** | | | | | | | | | | | | | | |
| **10** | | | | | | | | | | | | 3A ⌒ 3A | |

**System 2**

| | G7 | | C | | G7 | | C | | F | | C | | |
|---|---|---|---|---|---|---|---|---|---|---|---|---|---|
| **1** | (2) | (2) | (3) | (2) | (2) | (2) | (3) | (4) | (2) | (2) | (2) | (2) | (2) | (3) | (2) |
| **2** | | | | | | | | | | 8 | | | | 8 |
| **3** | | | 3B | | | | | | | | | | | |
| **4** | 3 | 3 | 3 | 3 | 3 | 3 | 1 | | 8 | | | 8 | 3 | 3 | 8 |
| **5** | 3 | 3 | 3A | | 3A 3A 4A | 3 | 3 | 1A 1A | | 8A | | 8A 8A | 3A | 3A | 3A |
| **6** | 3 | 3 | | | | 3 | 3 | 1 1 | 3B ⌒ 3B | | 8B 8B | 8B | | 3B |
| **7** | | | | | | | | | | | | | | |
| **8** | | | | | | | | 1 | 3 ⌒ 3 | | 8 | | | |
| **9** | | | | | | | | | | | | | | |
| **10** | | | | | | | | | 3A ⌒ 3A | | 8A | | | |

**System 3**

| | F | | C | | G7 | | C | | G7 | | C | | G7 | | C | | |
|---|---|---|---|---|---|---|---|---|---|---|---|---|---|---|---|---|---|
| **1** | (2) | (2) | (2) | (2) | (3) | (2) | | (2) | (2) | (2) | (2) | (3) | (2) | (2) | (2) | (2) | (4) | (2) |
| **2** | | | | | | | | | | | | | | | | |
| **3** | | | | | | | | | | | | 3B | | | | |
| **4** | | | 8 | 3 | 3 | 3 | | 3 | 3 | 3 | 3 | 3· | 3 | 3 | 3 | 1 | |
| **5** | 8A | | 8A 8A | 3A | 3A | 3 | 3A | 3A | 3A | 3 | 3 | 3 · | 3A 3A 4A | 3 | 3 | 1A 1A | |
| **6** | 8B | 8B | 8B | | 3B | 3 | 3B | | | 3 | 3 | | | 3 | 3 | 1 1 | 3B ⌒ 3B |
| **7** | | | | | | | | | | | | | | | | |
| **8** | | 8 | | | | | | | | | | | | | 1 | 3 ⌒ 3 |
| **9** | | | | | | | | | | | | | | | | |
| **10** | | 8A | | | | | | | | | | | | | 3A ⌒ 3A |

# Little Liza Jane

Arr. Dewitt Scott

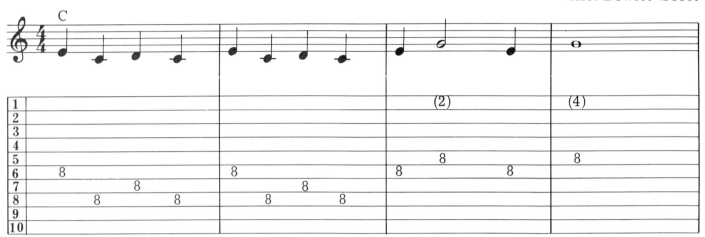

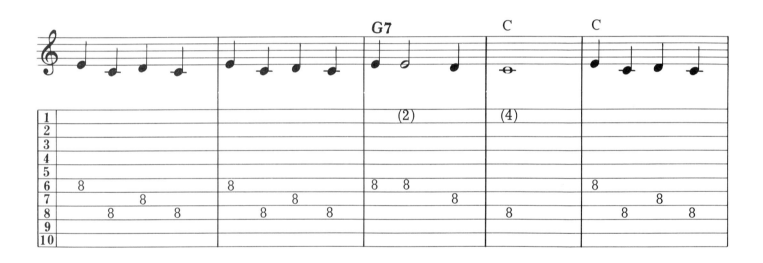

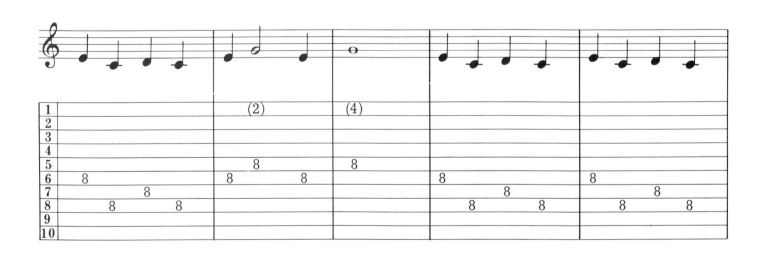

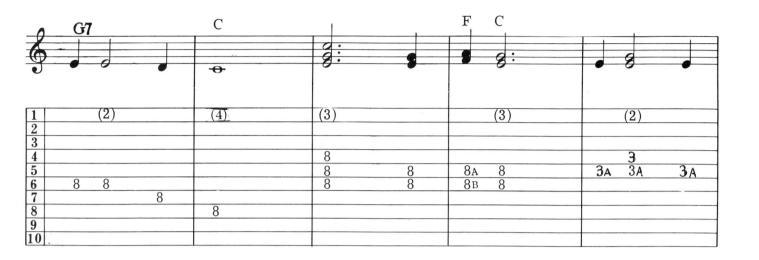

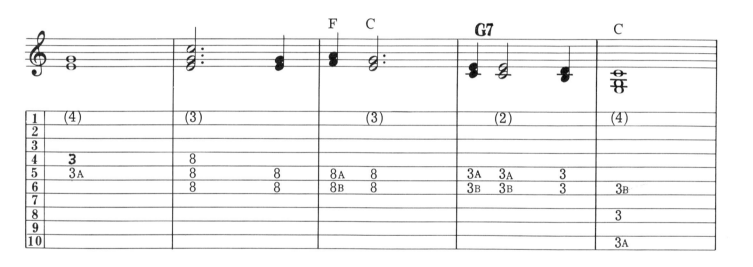

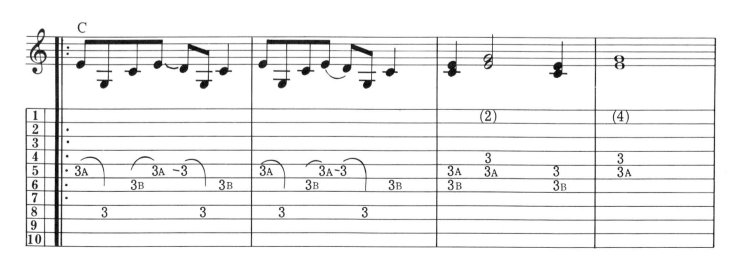

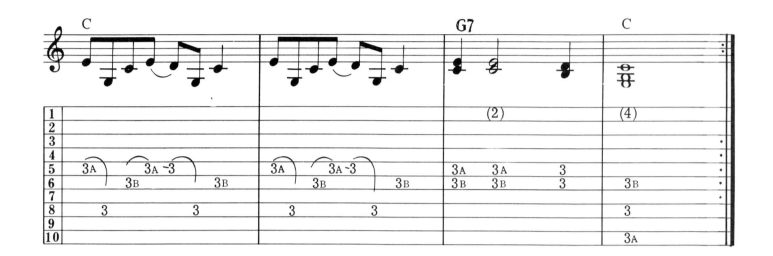

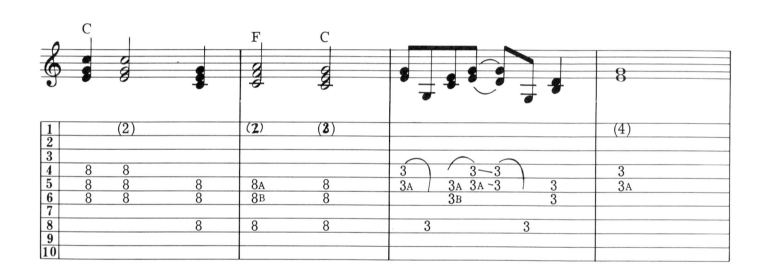

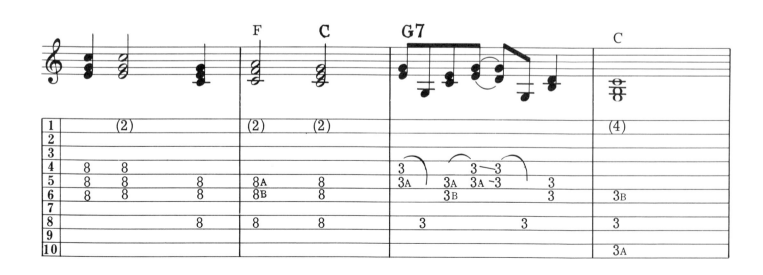

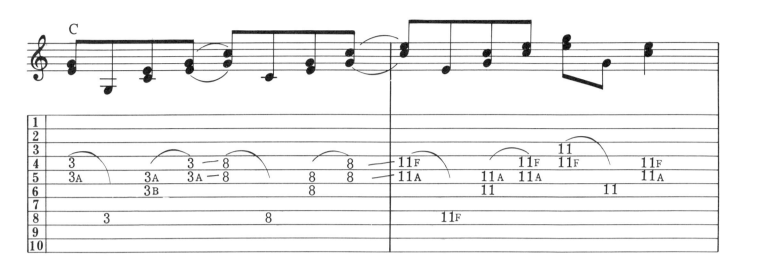

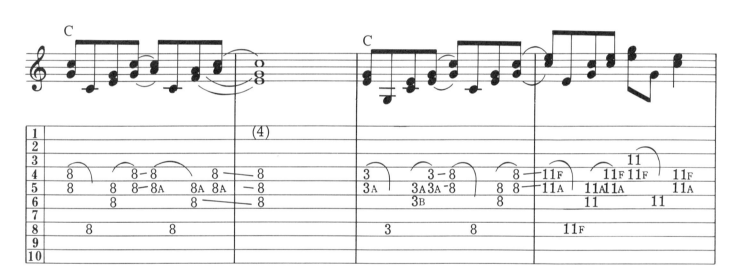

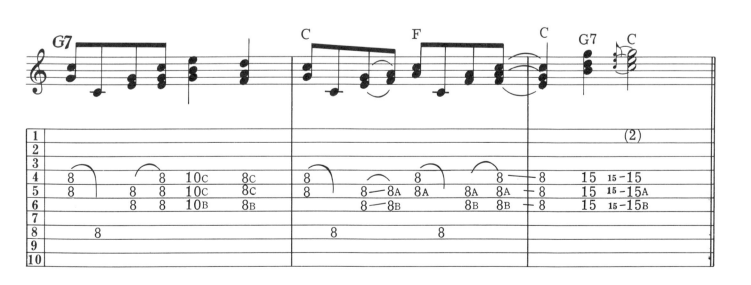

# Pedal Drag

Dewitt Scott

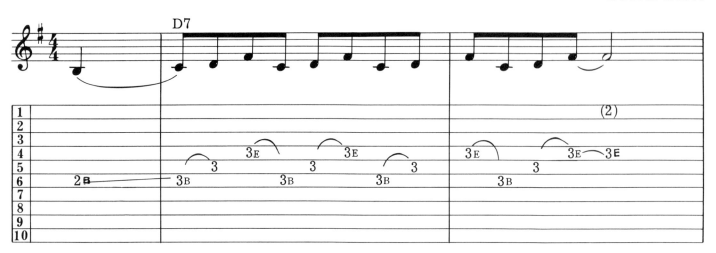

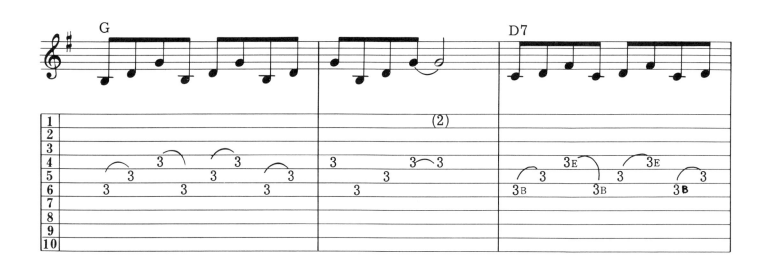

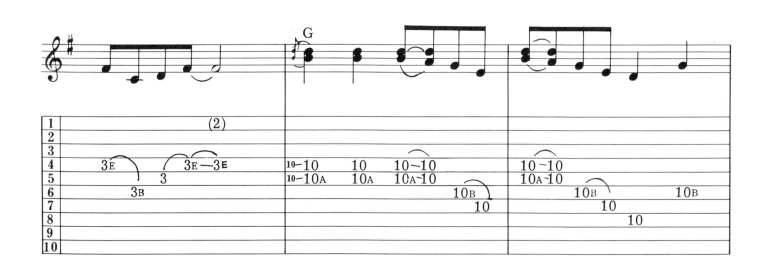

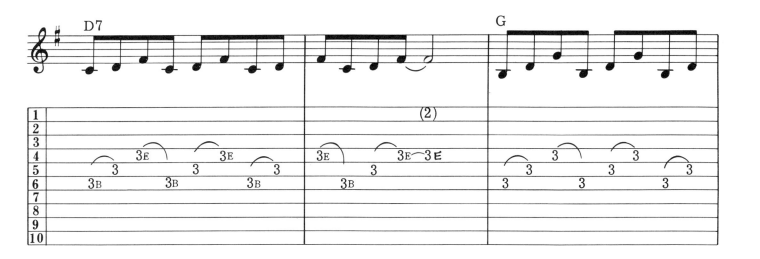

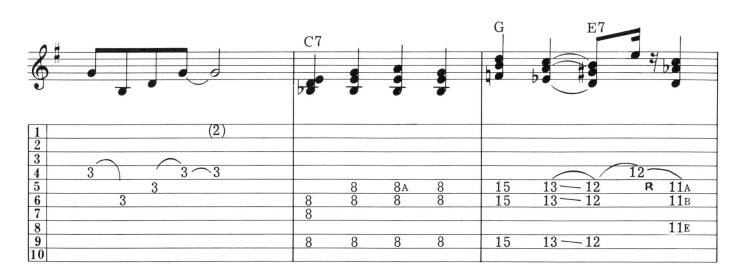

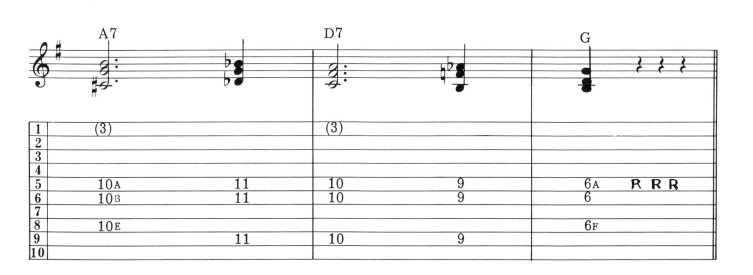

# Waltz Of The Yukon

Dewitt Scott

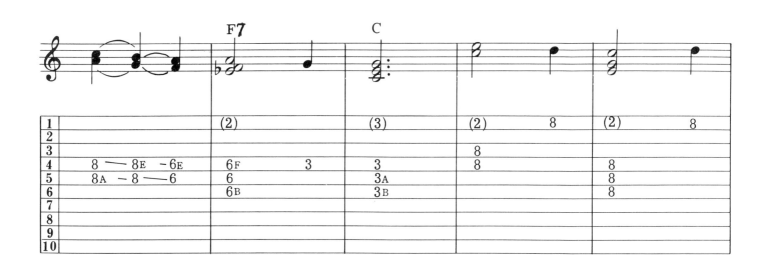

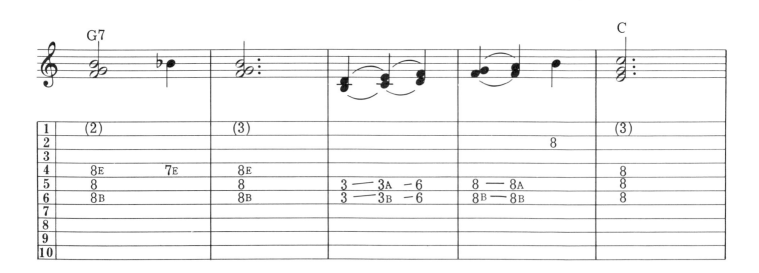

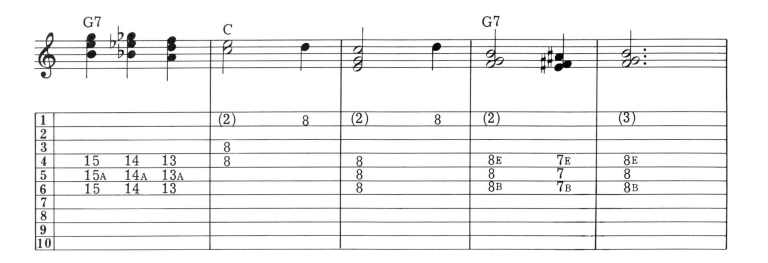

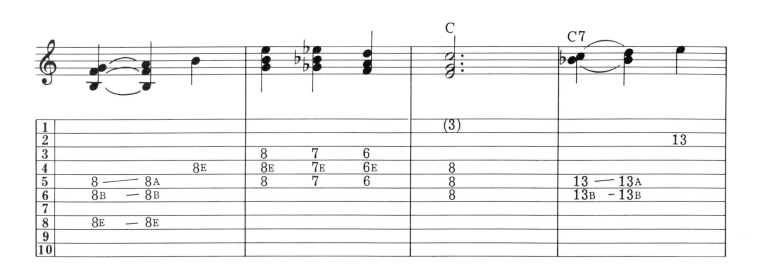

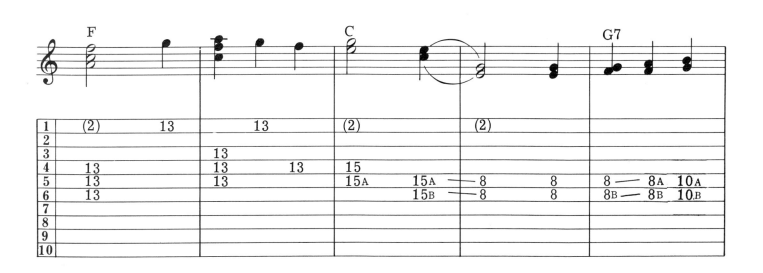

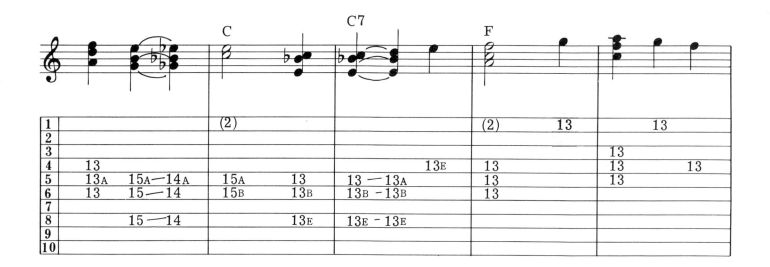

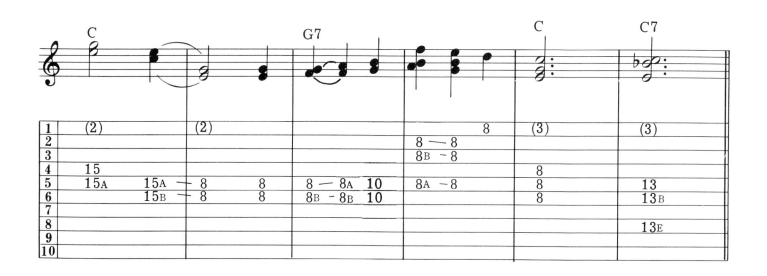

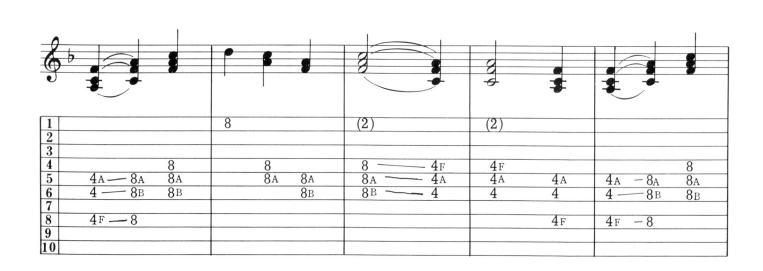

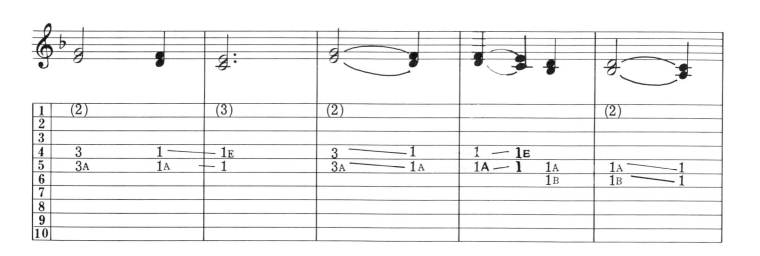
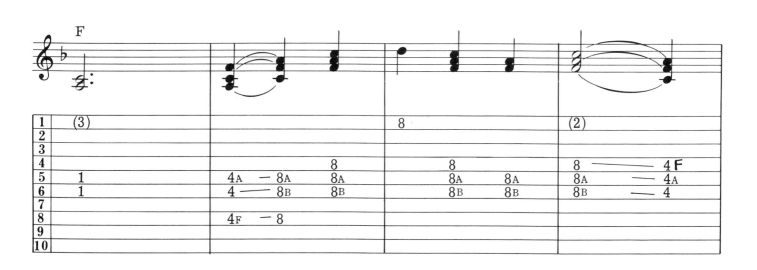

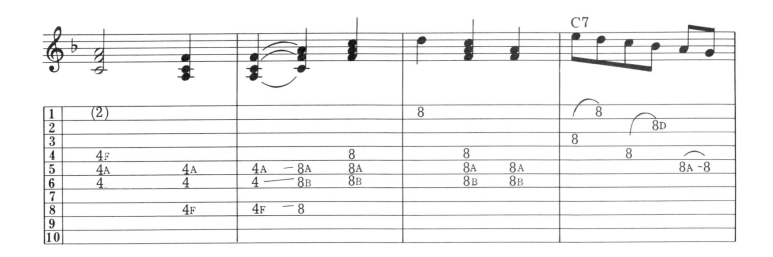

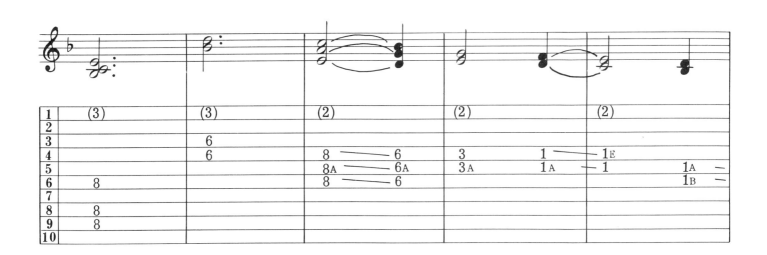

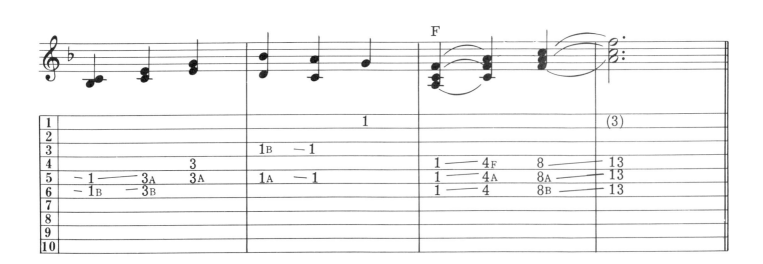

Jim Murphy

Buddy Cage

Joe Goldmark

Janne Lindgren
—Sweden

# Amazing Grace

Arranged by Dewitt Scott

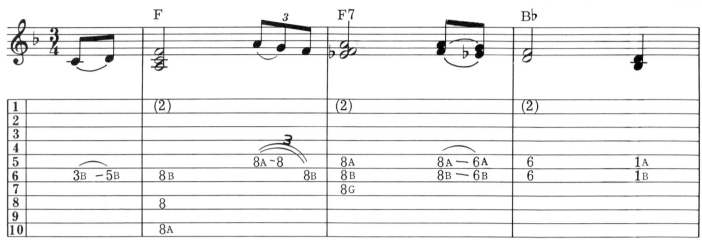

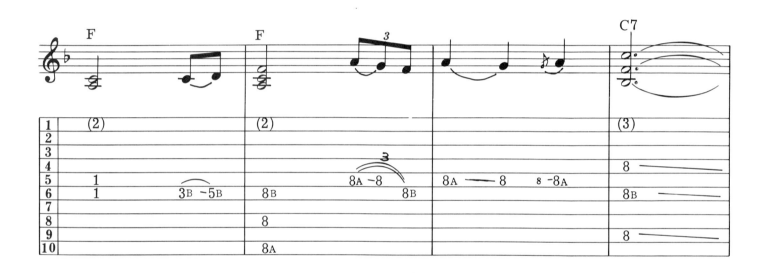

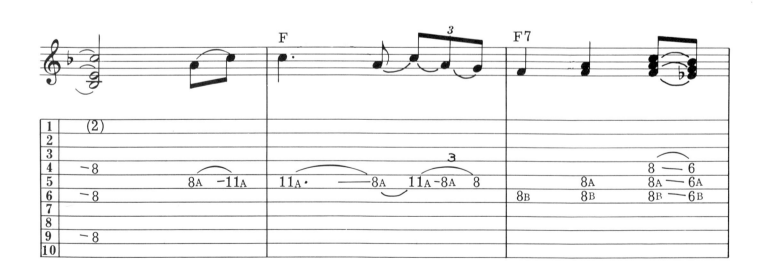

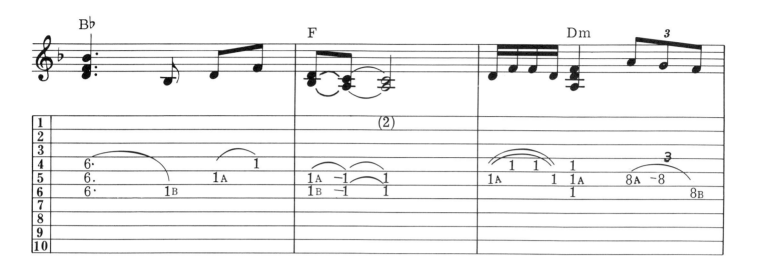

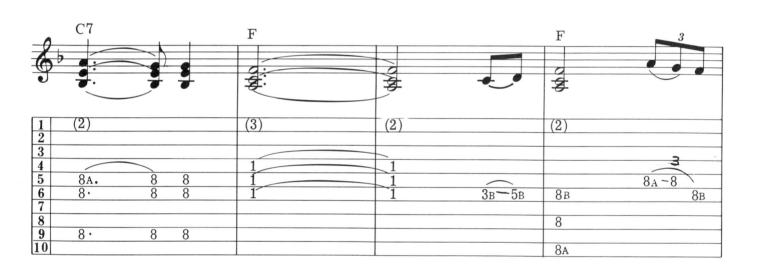

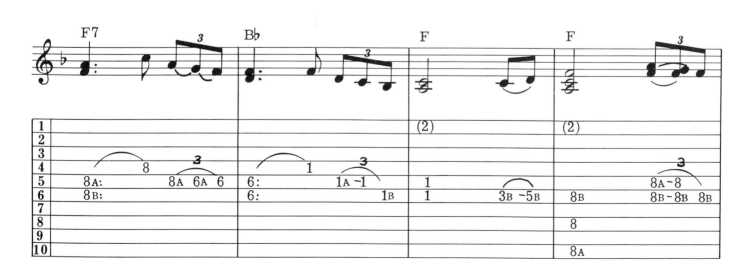

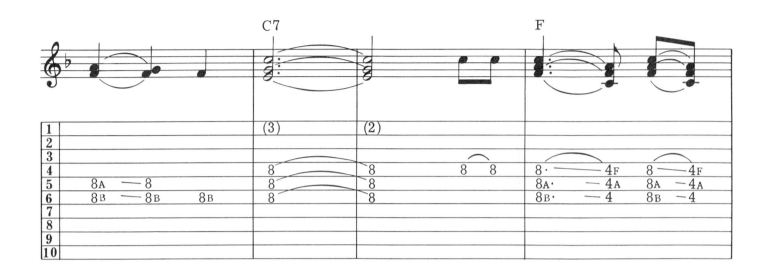

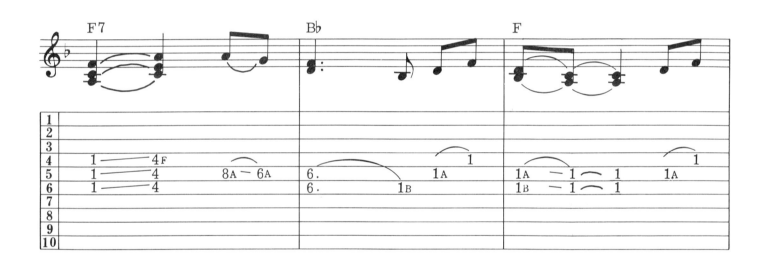

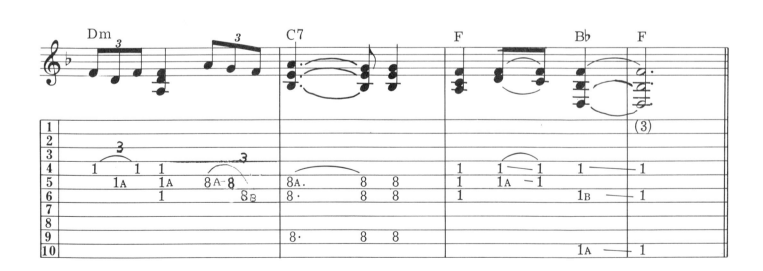

**Paul Franklin**

**Pete Drake**

**Johnny Cox**

# Ozark Ramble

Dewitt Scott

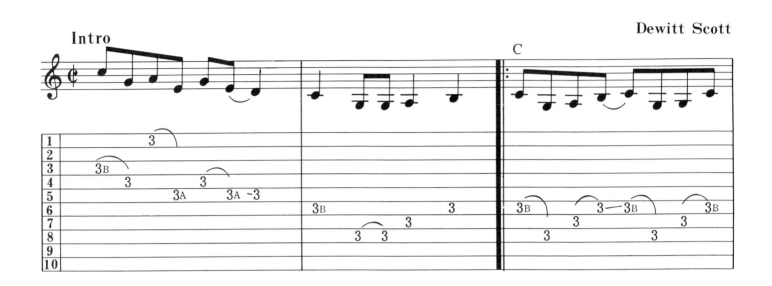

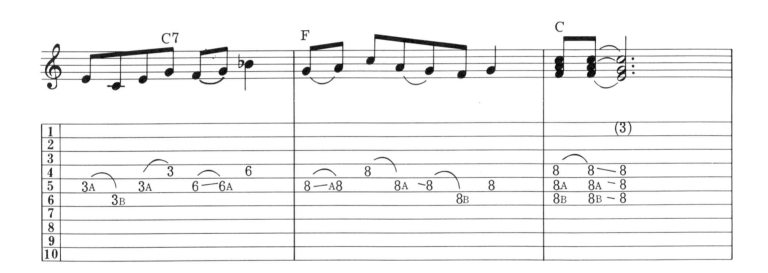

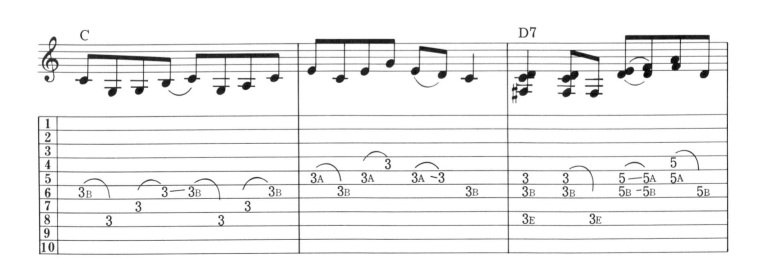

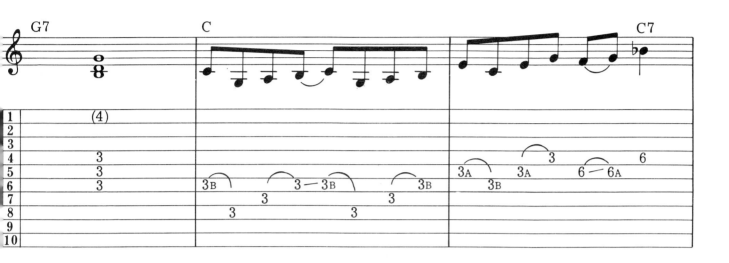

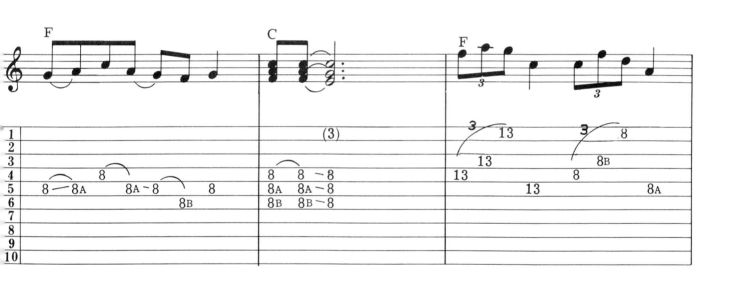

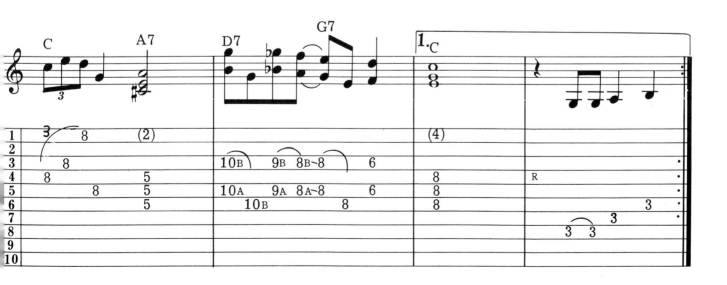

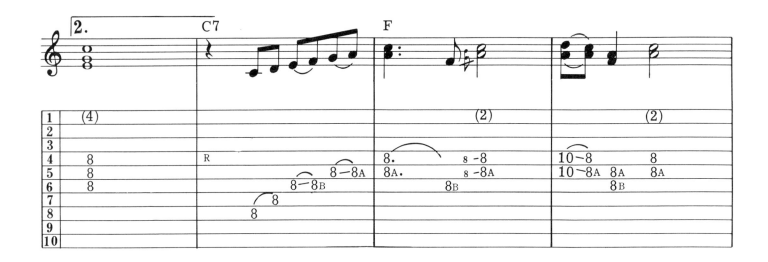

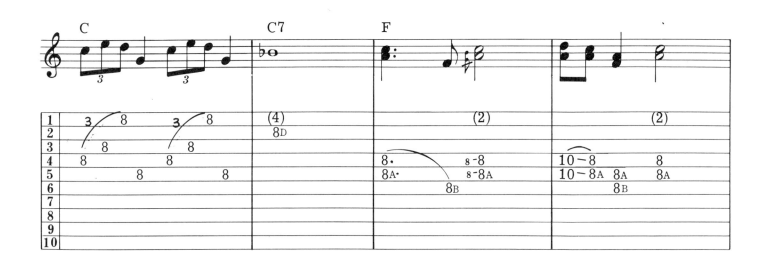

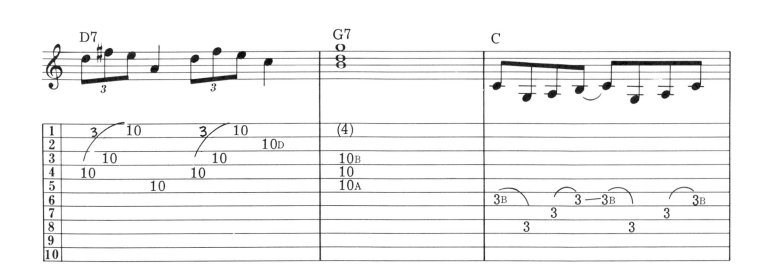

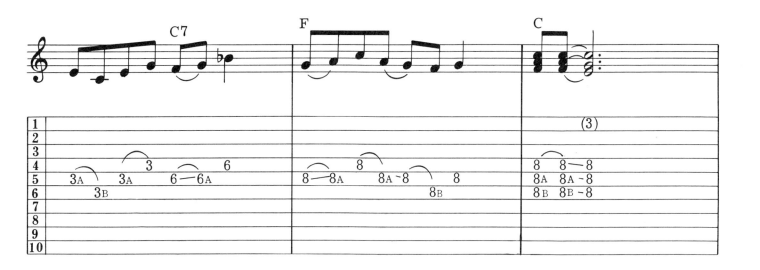

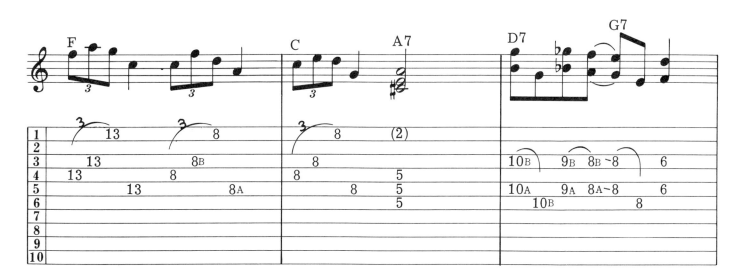

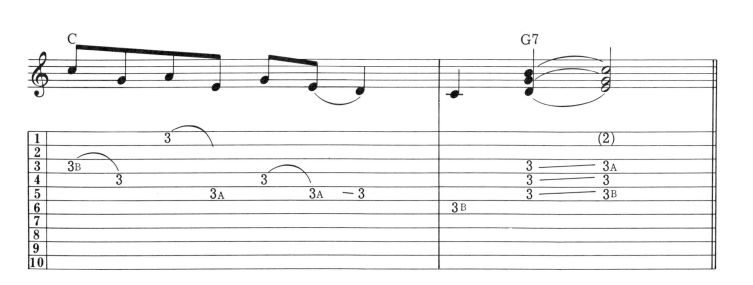

# Greensleeves

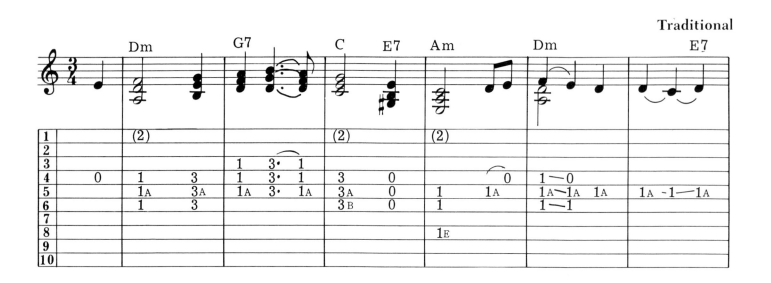

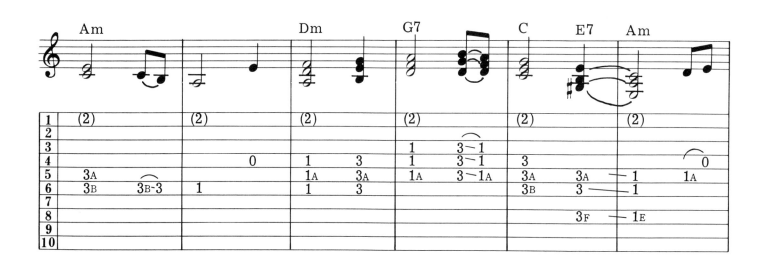

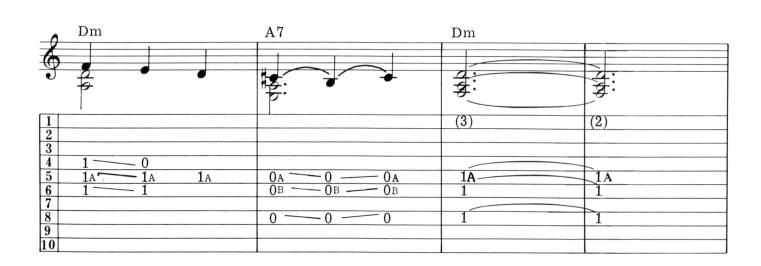

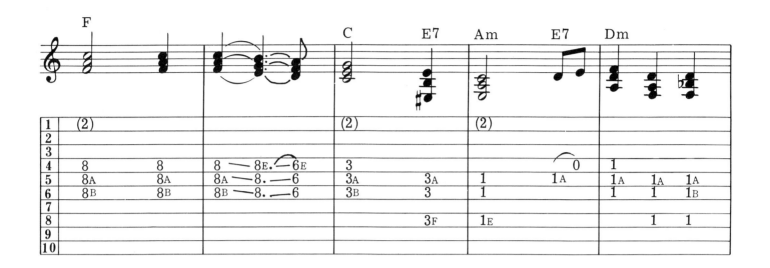

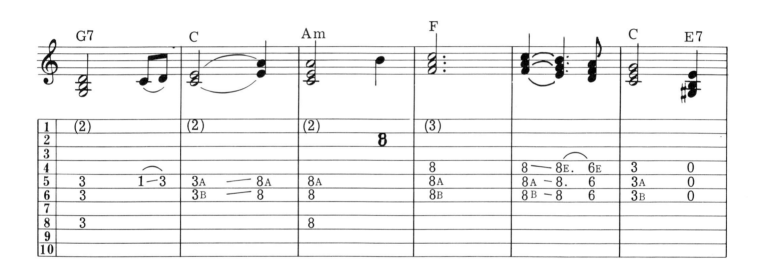

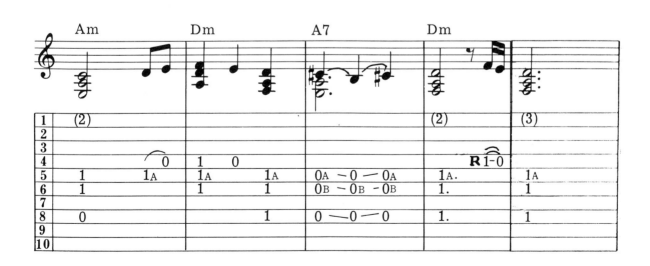

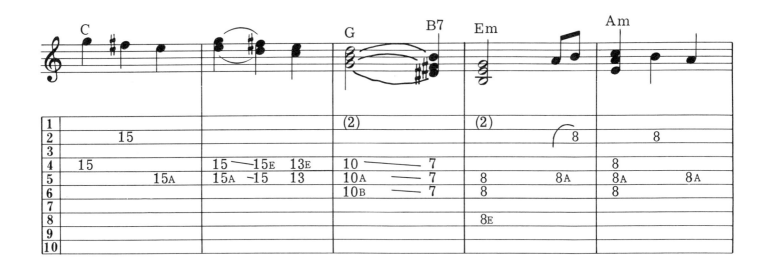

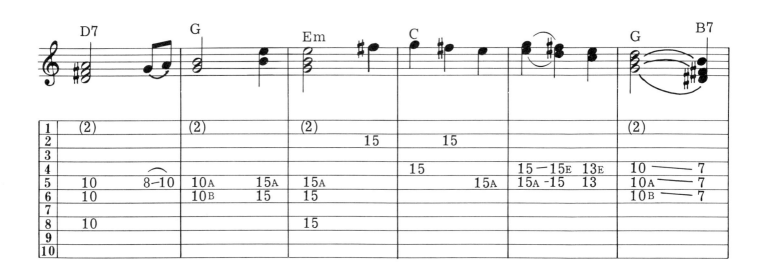

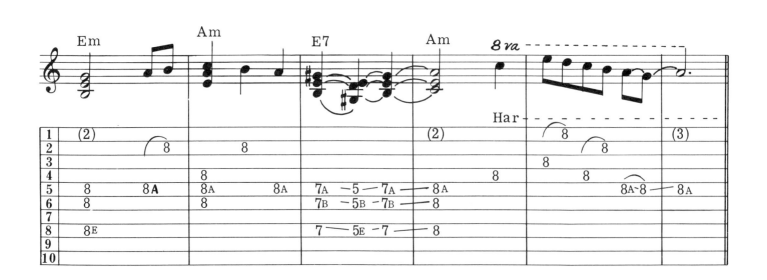

# Fast Finger Exercises

Learn to play as fast as possible using all three fingers.

Finger pattern

T  =  Thumb

•  =  1st finger

• •  =  2nd finger

Same fingering

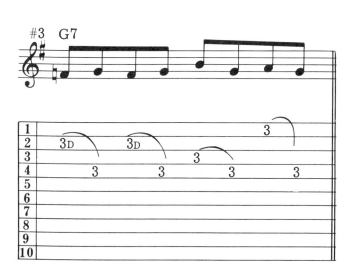

**Jeff Newman**

# Fast Picking

There is a new style of fast picking that has been introduced by the young steel guitarists in Nashville. Some players use all three fingers to execute this new style while others use the thumb and one finger. Start them slow and learn to play them as fast as you can.

## Three Fast Patterns

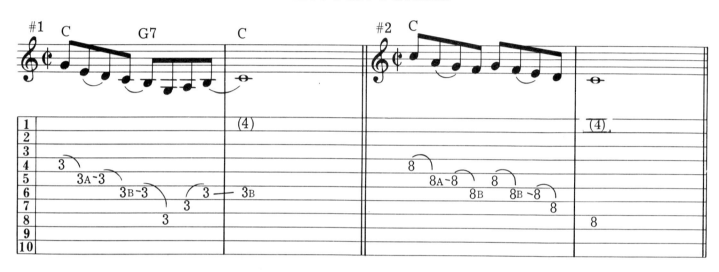

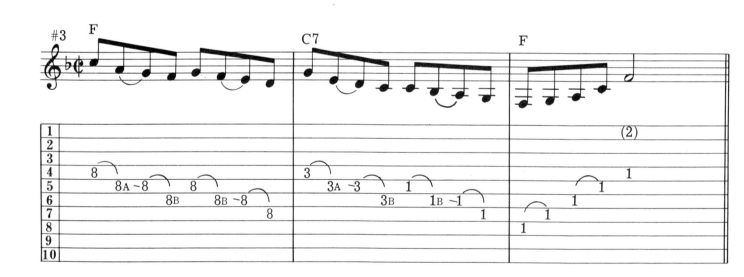

# A Very Good Run

This run works so well both as a fill behind a singer or can be used in solo work. Have the "A" pedal depressed on the first measure for the 18's and again on all the 6's in measure 3.

8va---= Notes are to be played one octave higher.
(measures 1 and 2) notes only!

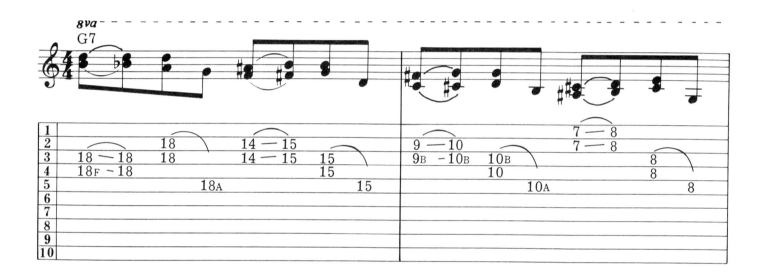

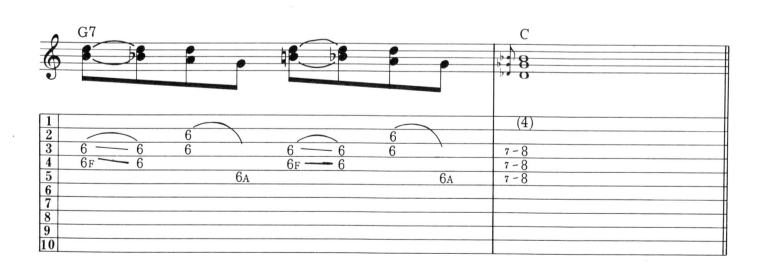

# Londonderry Aire
## H Knee Lever

**Traditional**

D-Knee Lever = Lower
2nd String Whole Tone

Used with Permission
from Album Buddy Emmons
ELP-1001 Emmons Guitar Co.
PO Box 1366 Burington, N.C. 27215

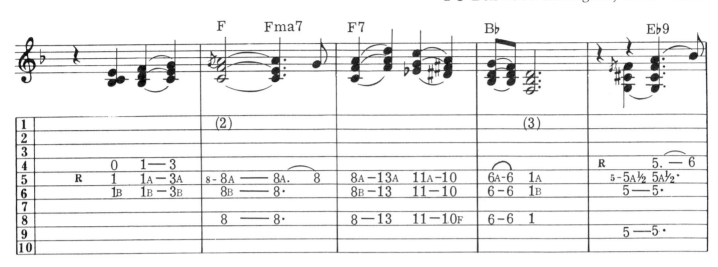

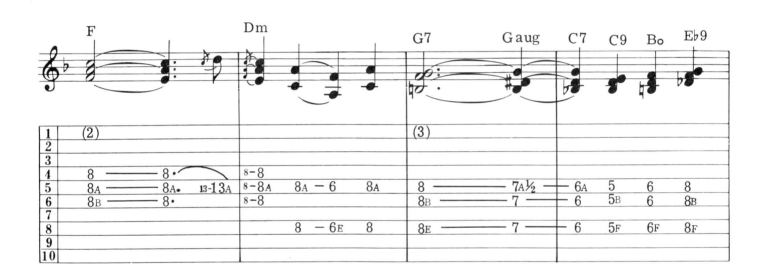

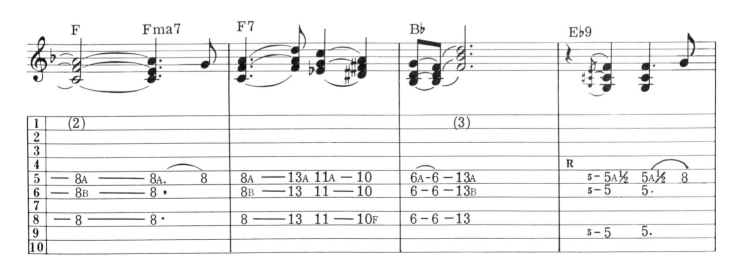

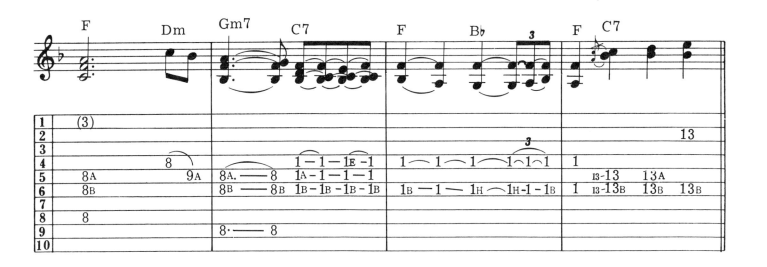

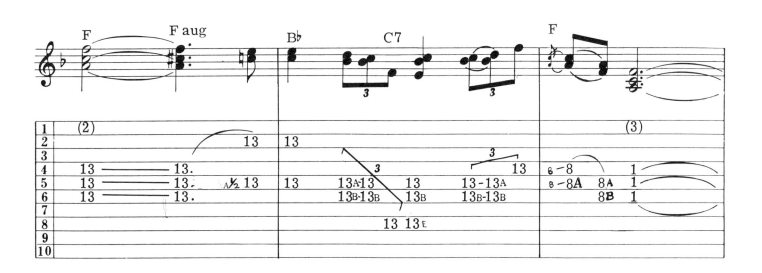

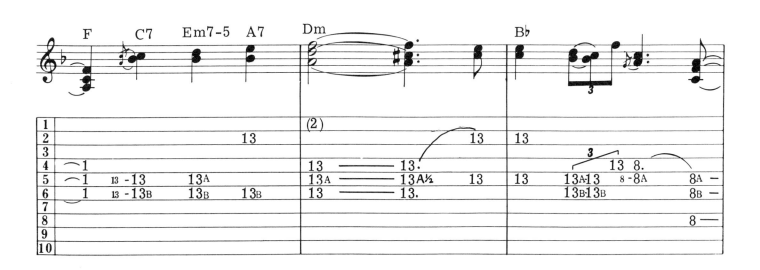

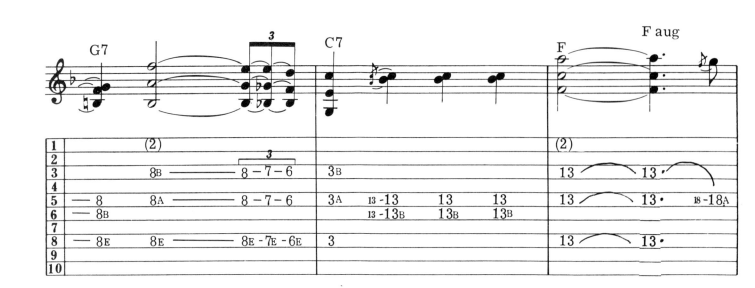

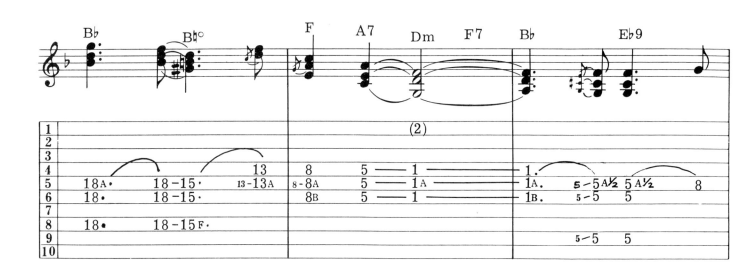

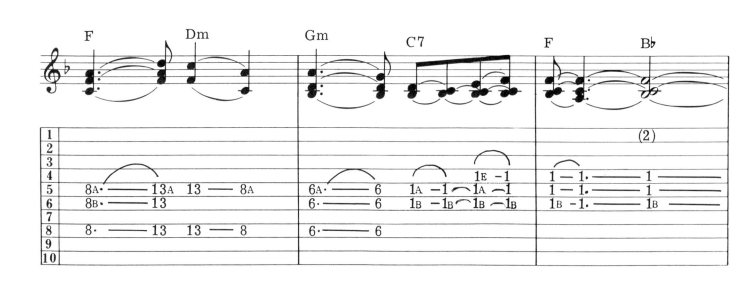

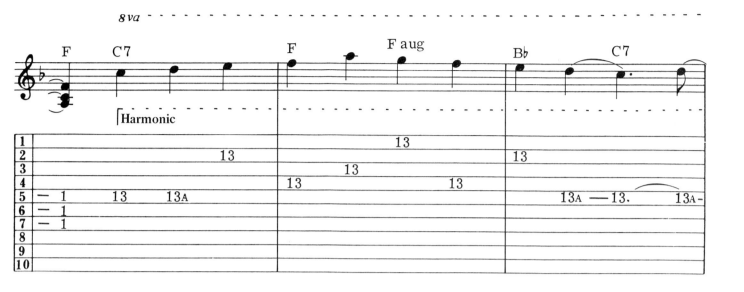

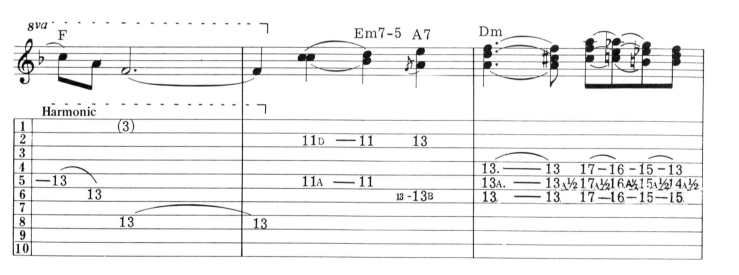

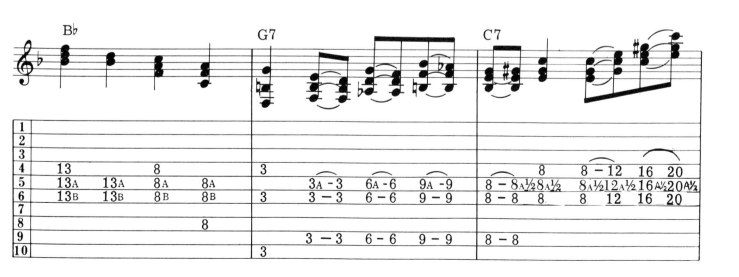

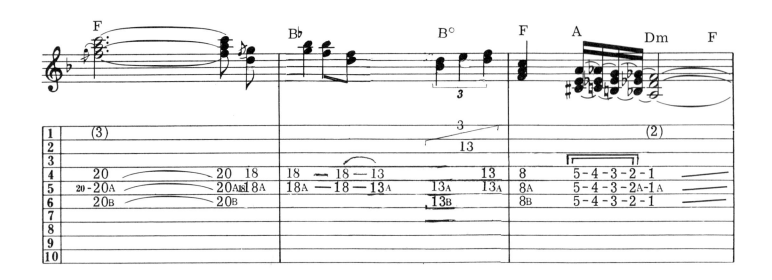

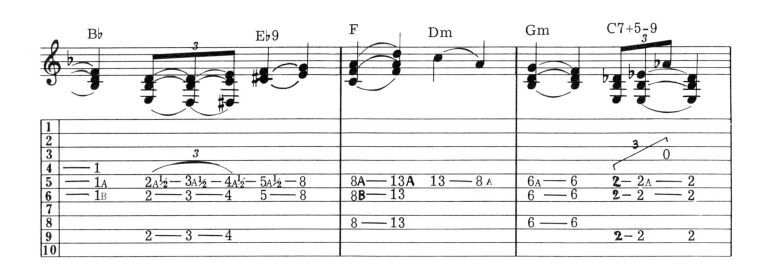

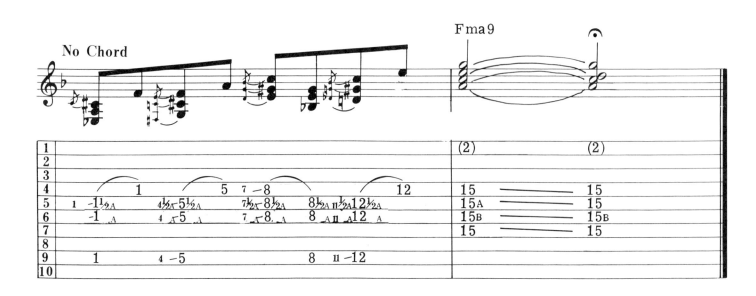

Jimmy Day

Curly Chalker

**Wesley W. "Speedy" West**

95

# Bars Of Steel

Used by Permission
from Album "Lloyd's of Nashville"
MD-28 P O Box 2581 St. Louis,
Mo.63114

by Lloyd Green

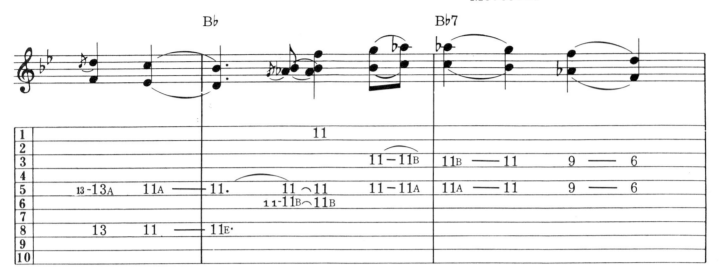

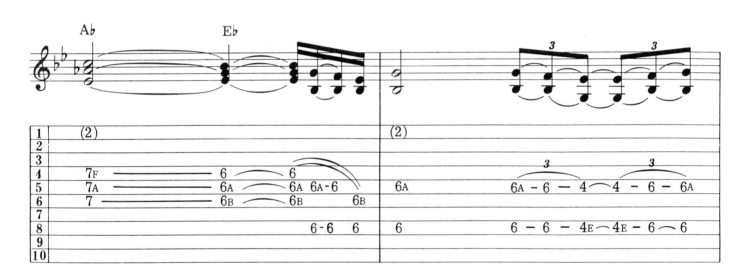

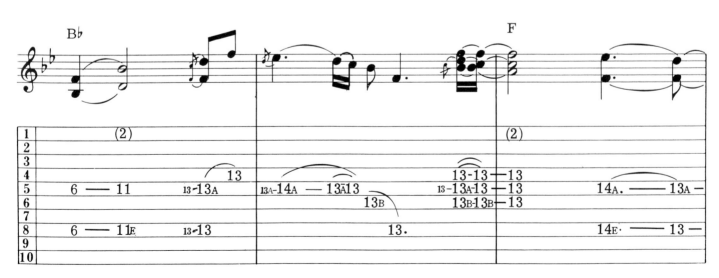

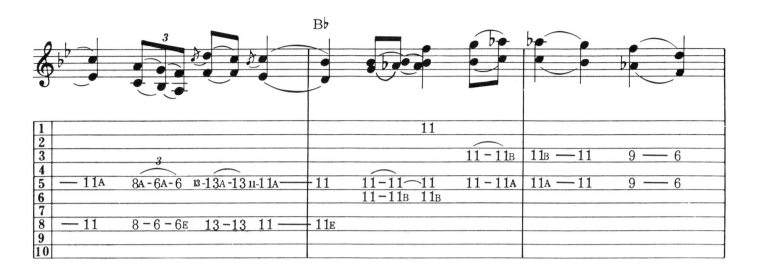

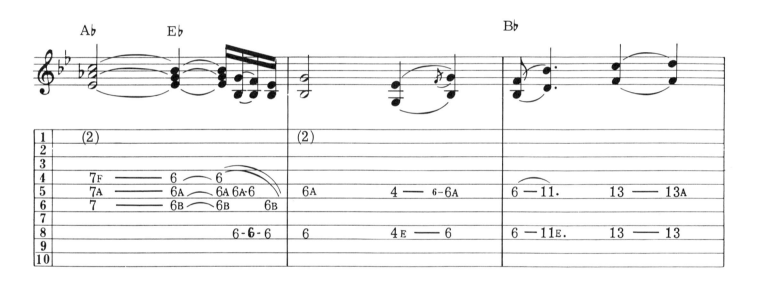

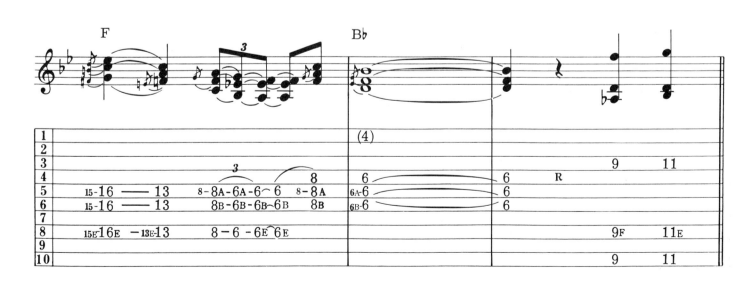

97

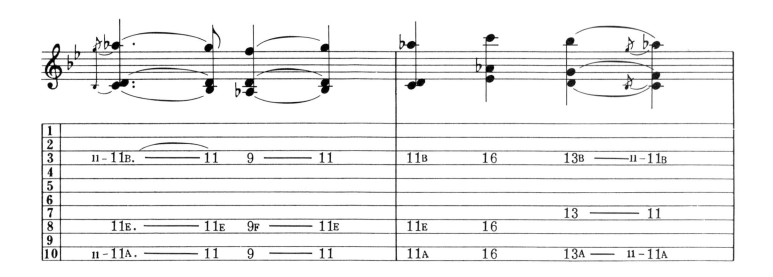

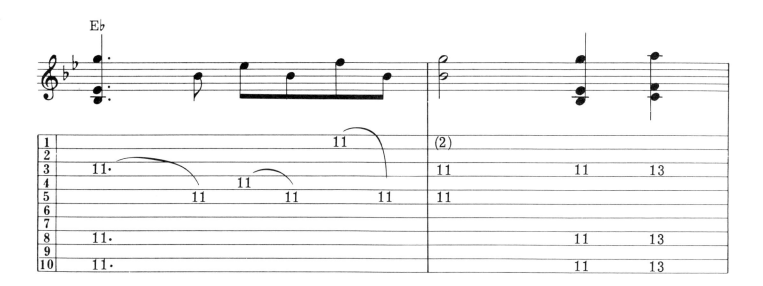

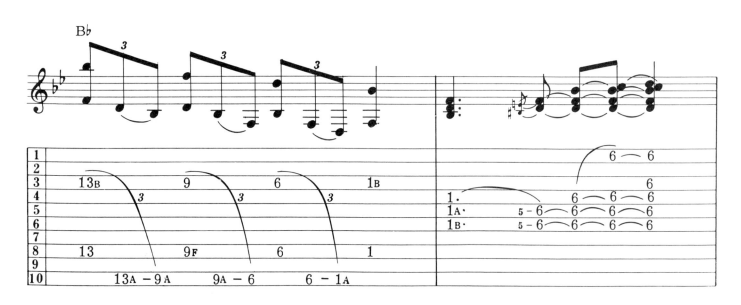

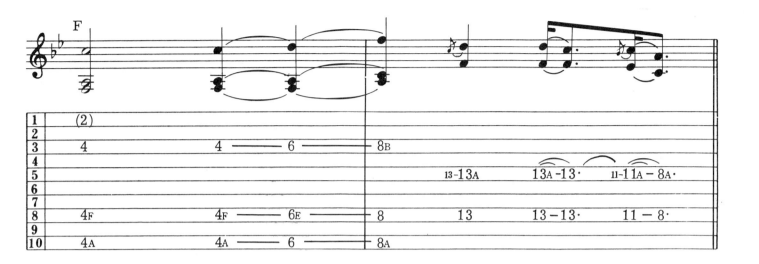

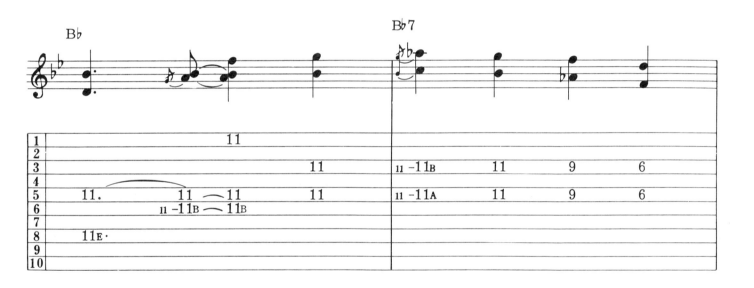

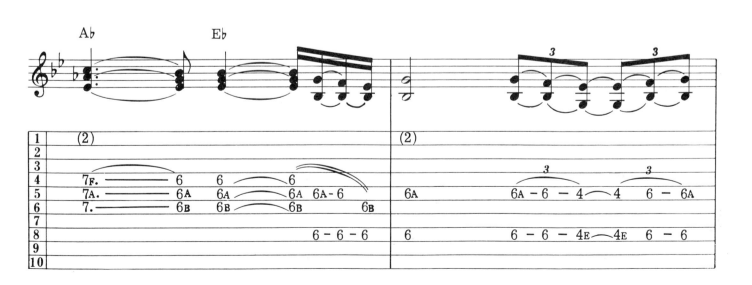

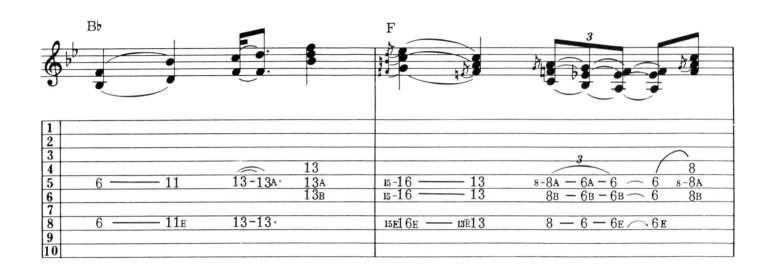

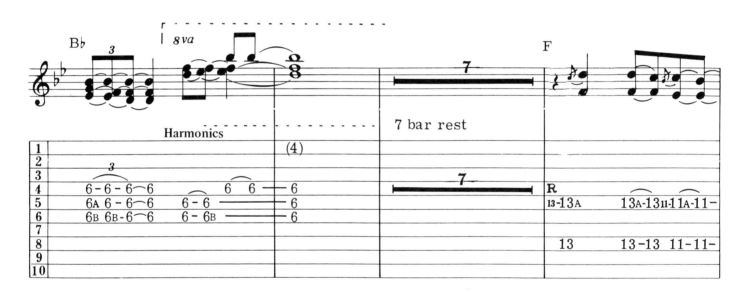

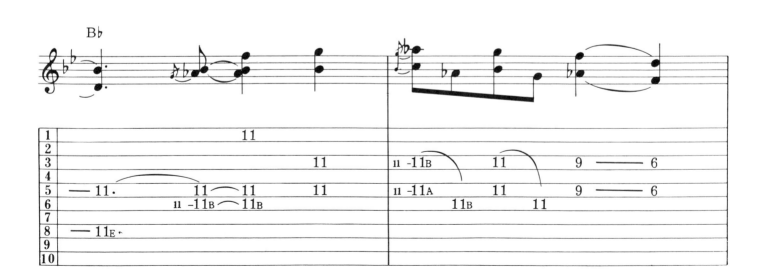

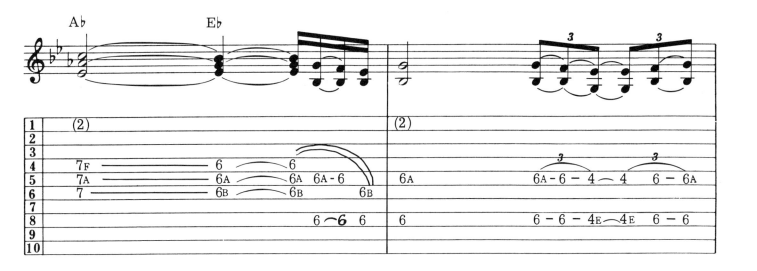

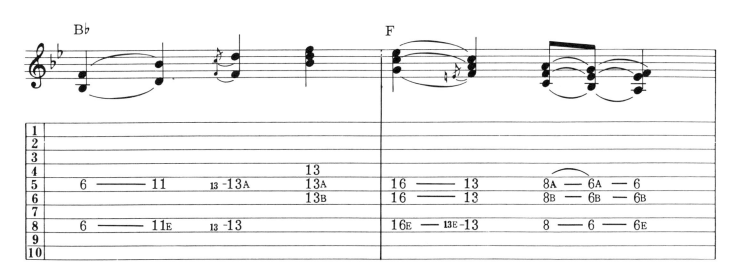

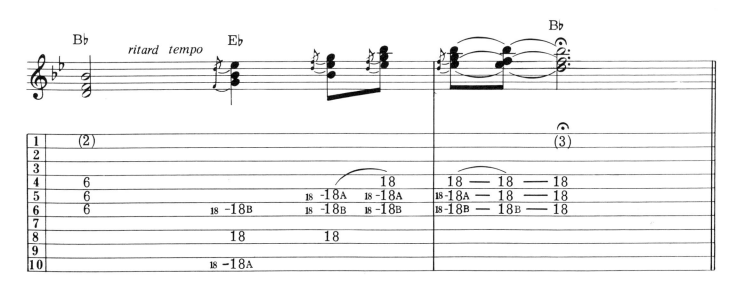

# Brown Baggin'

Music by Mike Smith
Tab by Russ Wever

Knee Lever L= Lower the
ninth string one fret

Used with Permission
from the Album "Dreams
of India" USR-1
524 Singer Dr.
Madison, TN. 37115

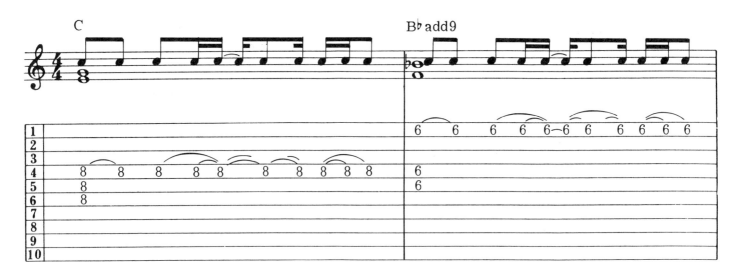

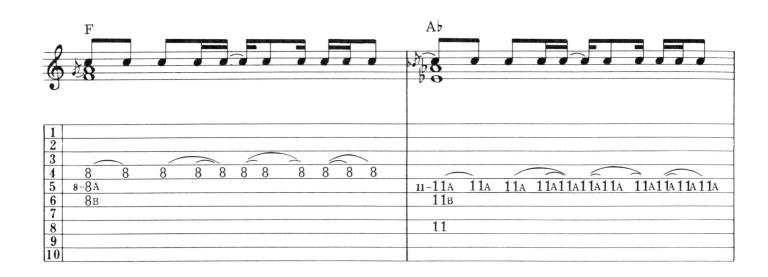

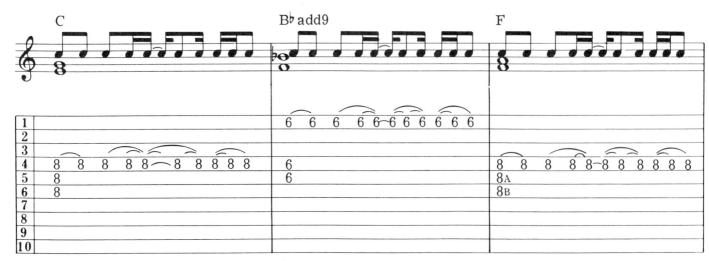

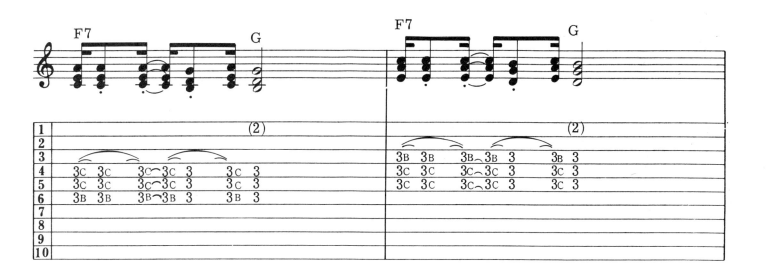

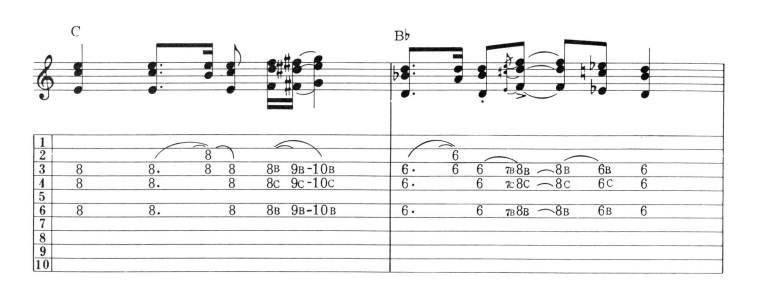

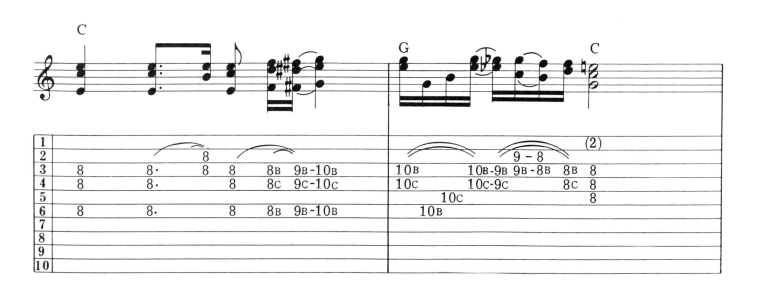

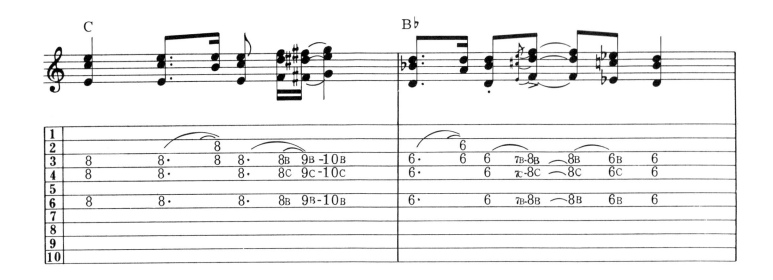
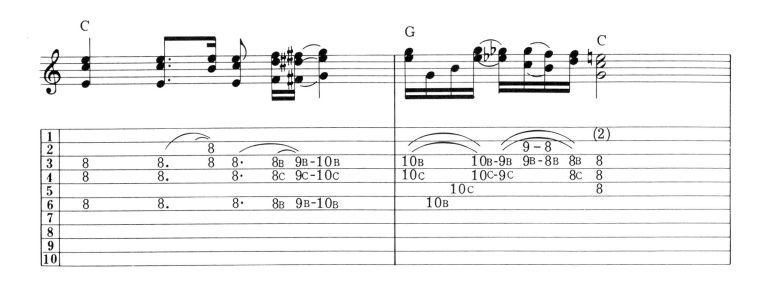
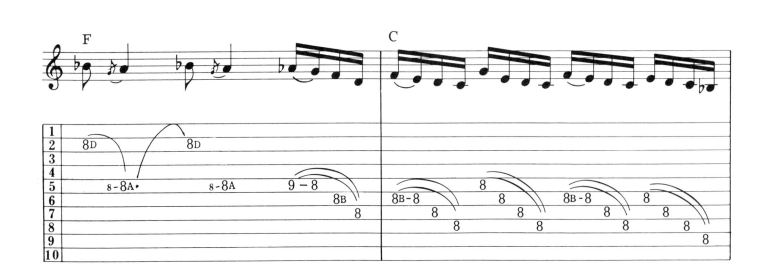

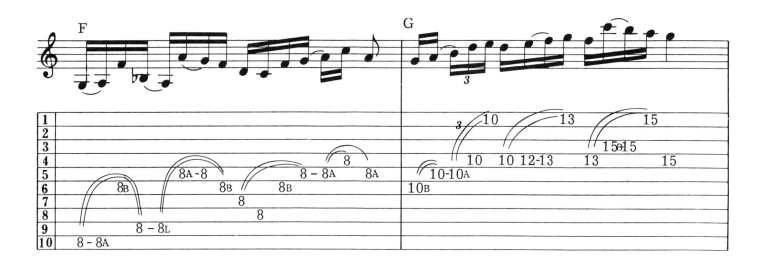

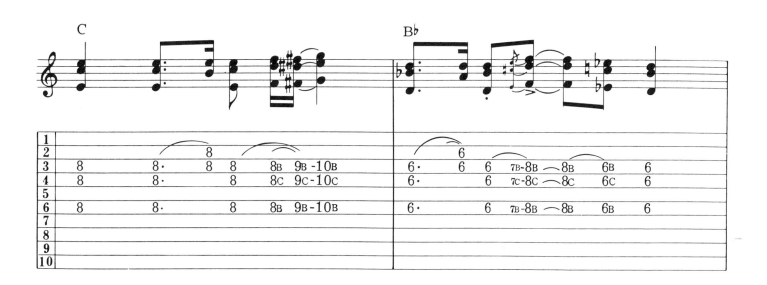

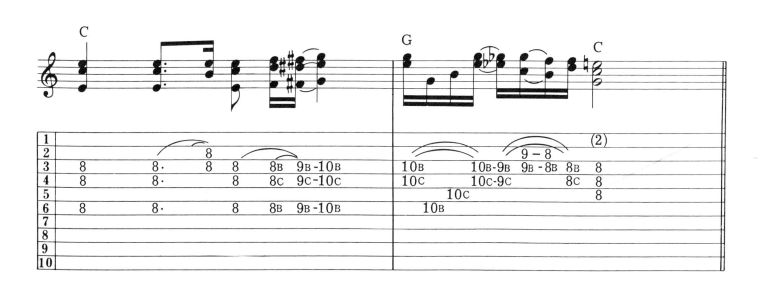

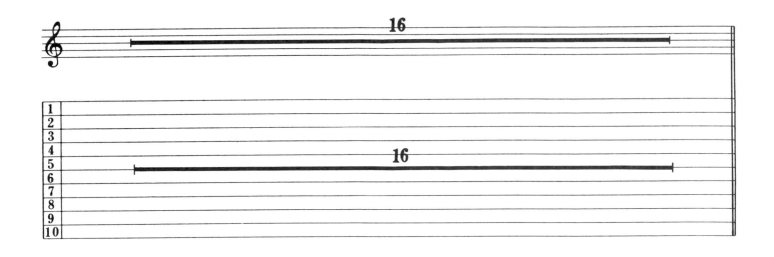

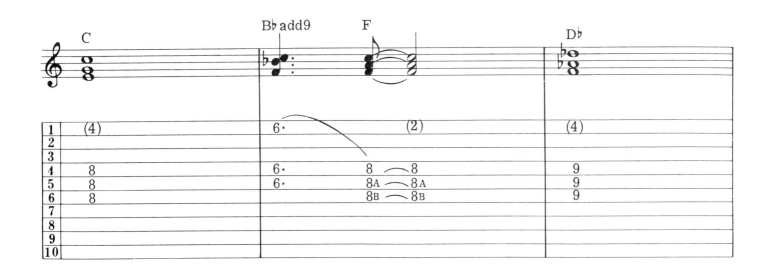

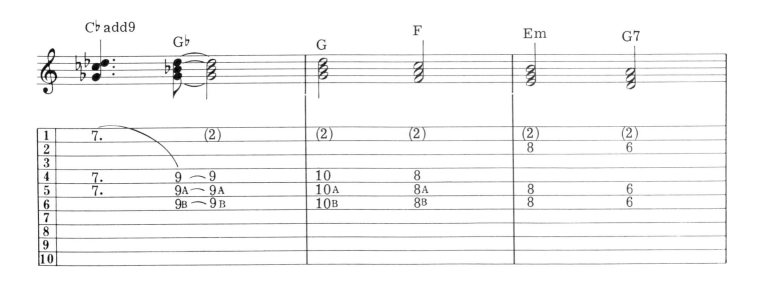

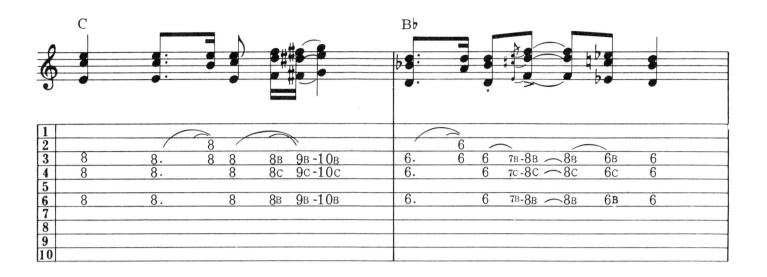

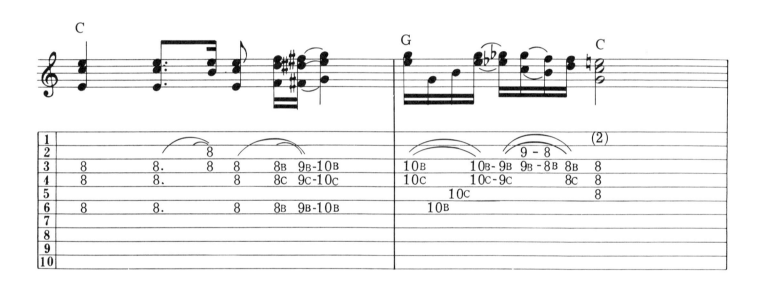

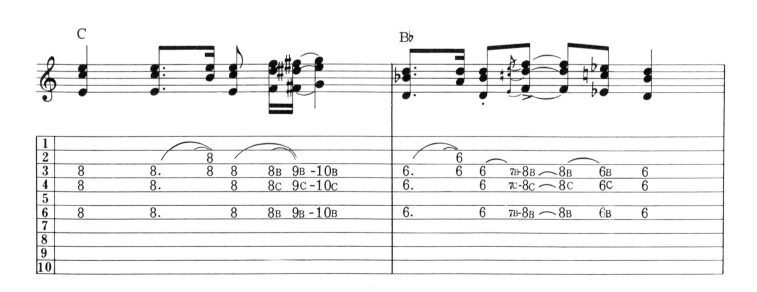

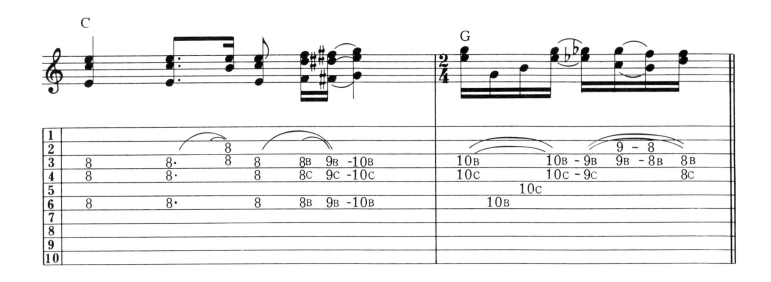

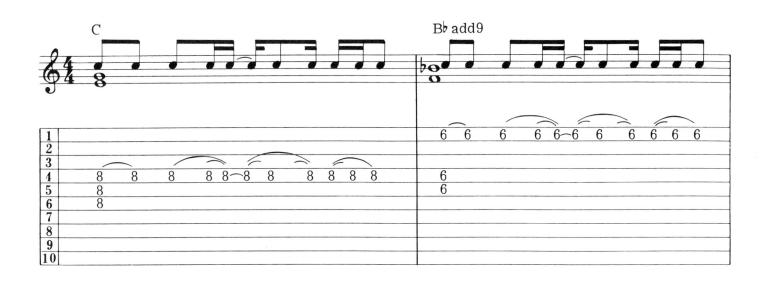

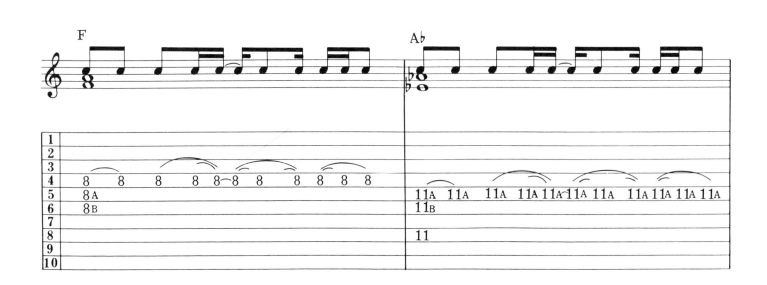

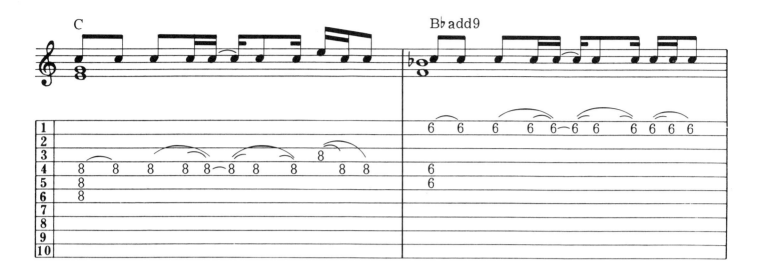

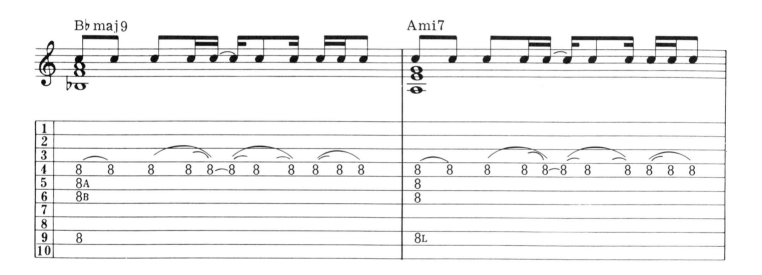

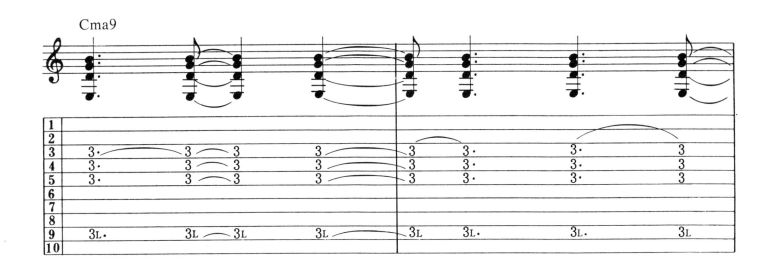

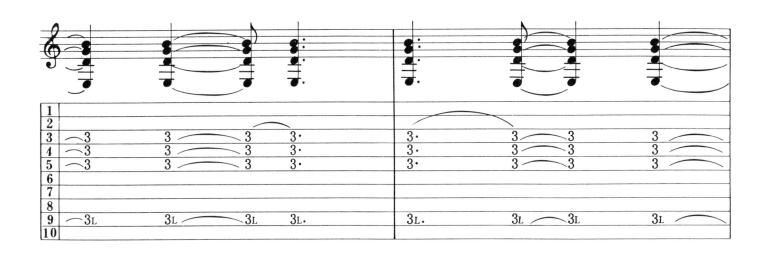

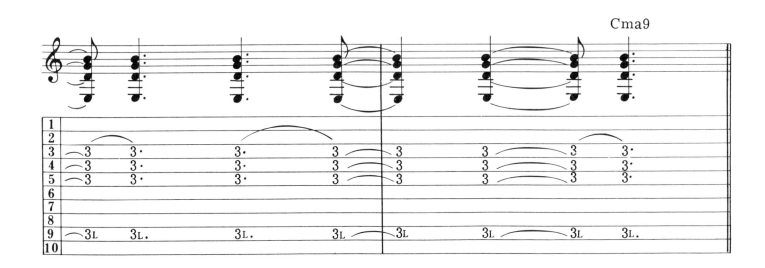

**Jay Dee Maness**

**Winnie Winston**

**Ben Joyner**
*—Australia*

**Russ Hicks**

# Hot Foot

Written by Weldon Myrick
Tab by Fred Amandola
Notation by Russ Wever

Used by Permission
from the Album MD-24
Pedal Man by Weldon Myrick
Mid-Land Records
PO Box 2581
Overland, Mo. 63114

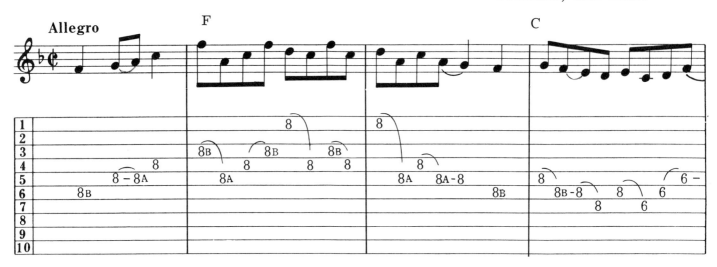

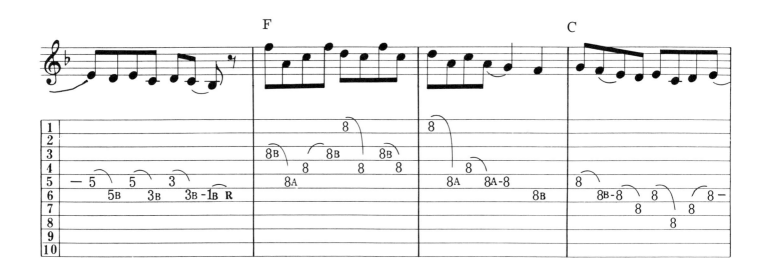

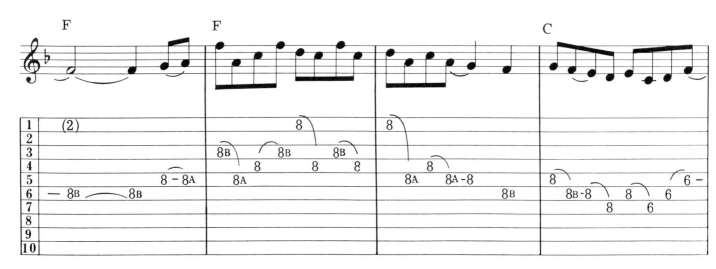

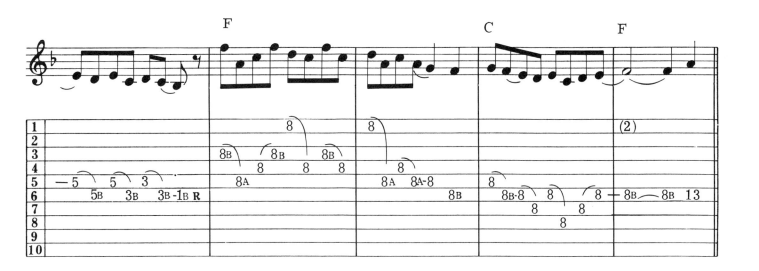

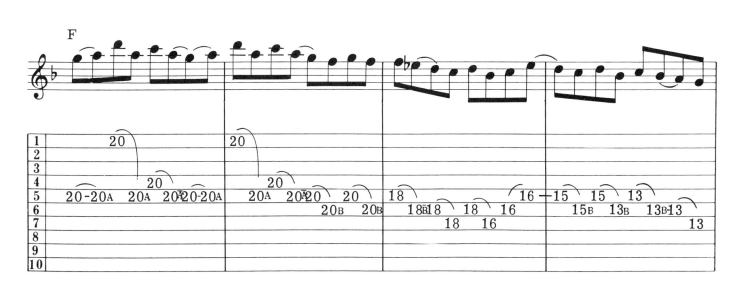

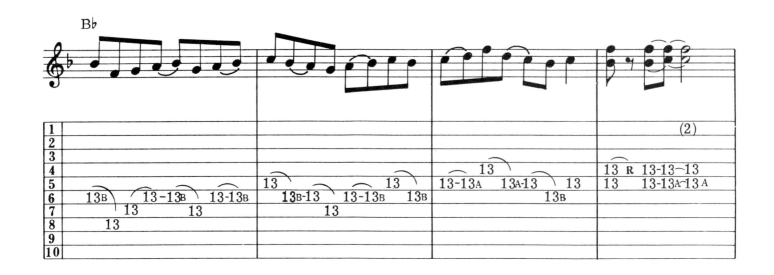

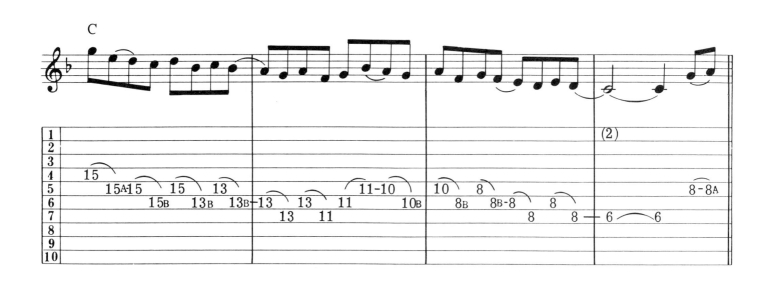

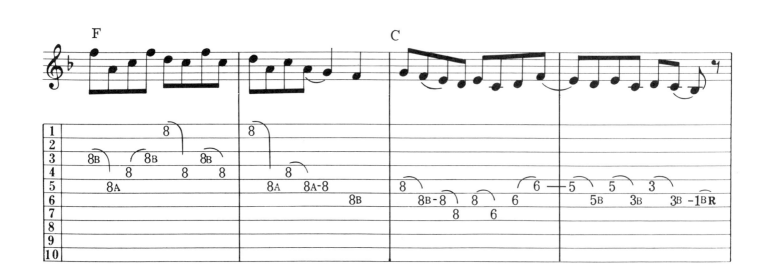

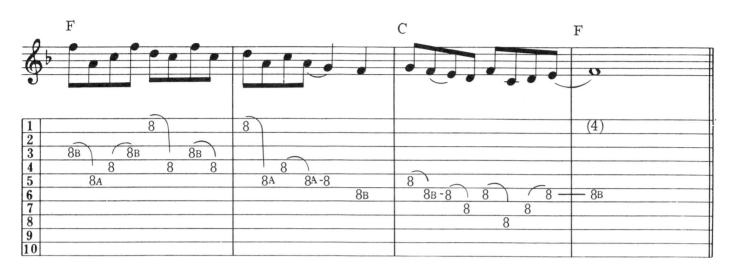

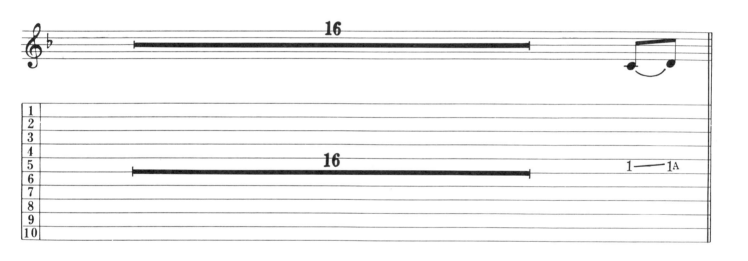

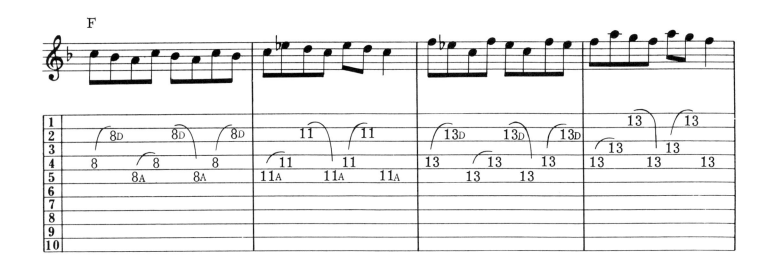

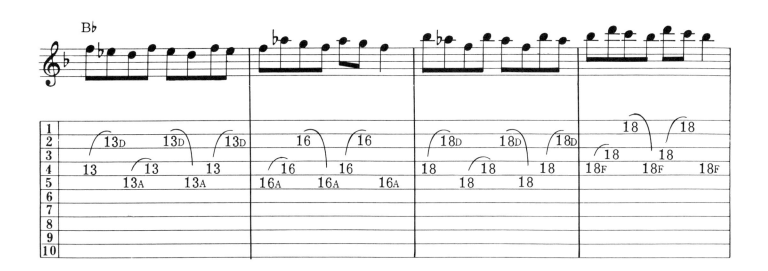

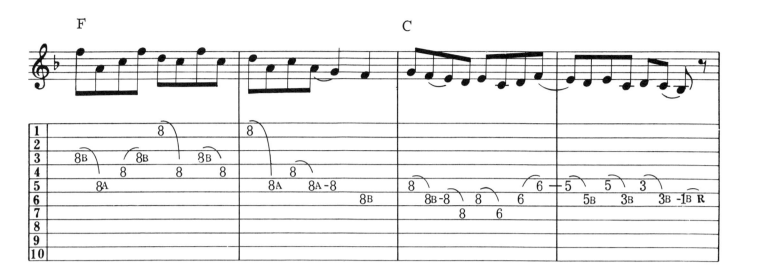

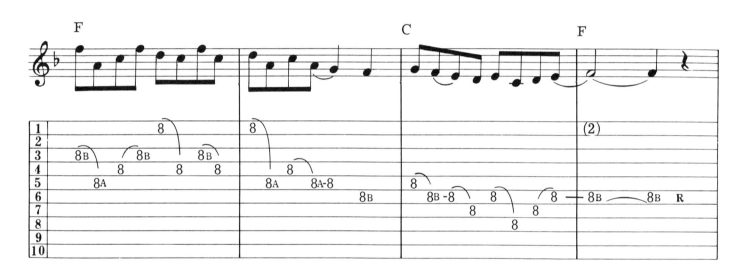

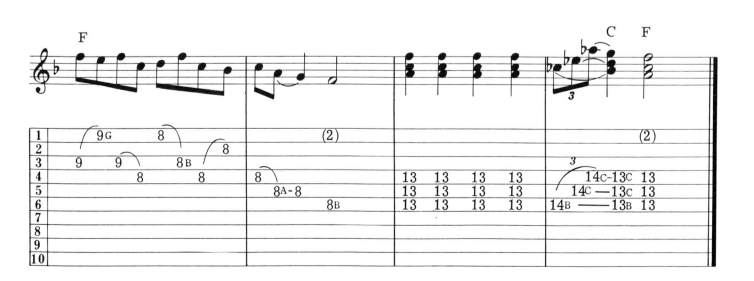

117

# Russian Rolls

Written by Nils Tuxen

**D Knee Lever = Lower
2nd String Whole Tone**

Used by Permission
from Album "United
Steels of Europe" Sonet
SLP 1565
Sonet/Dansk Grammofon A/S
40 St. Kongens Gade
DK-1264 Copenhagen K
Denmark

**Intro
Allegro**

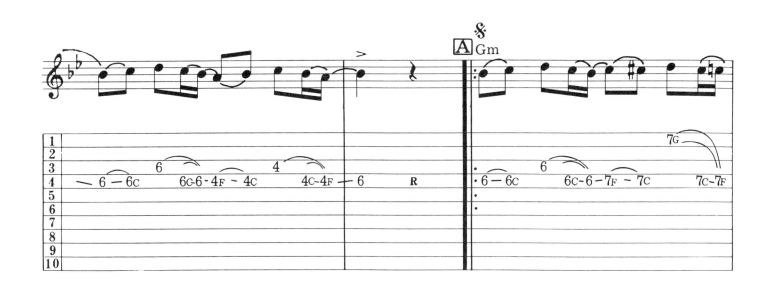

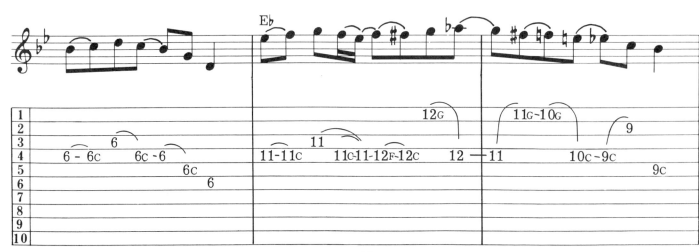

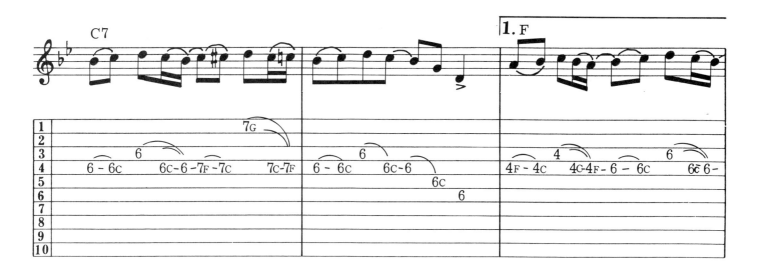

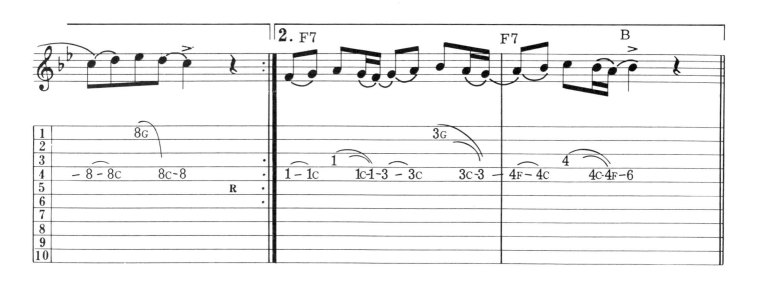

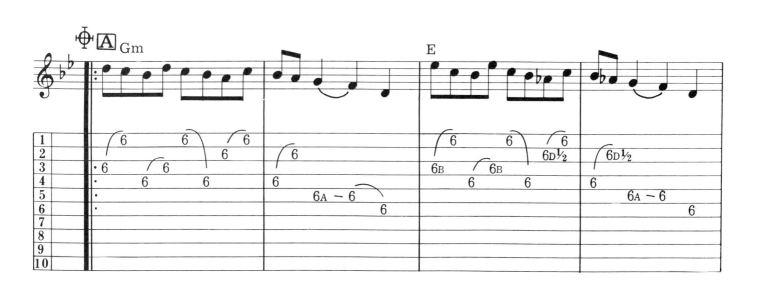

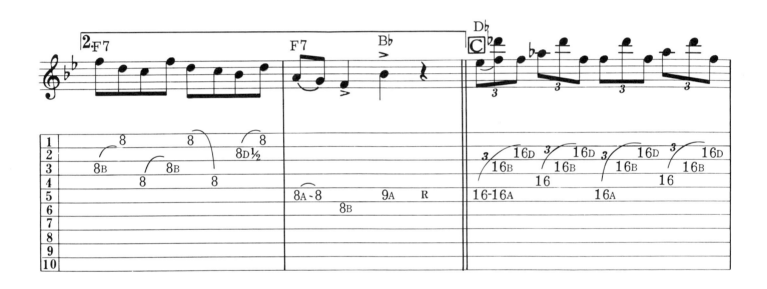

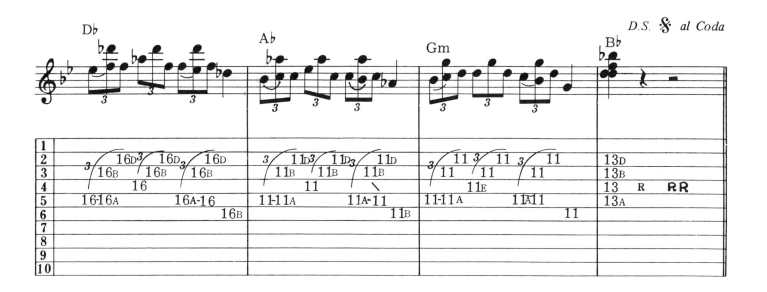

## ⊕ Coda

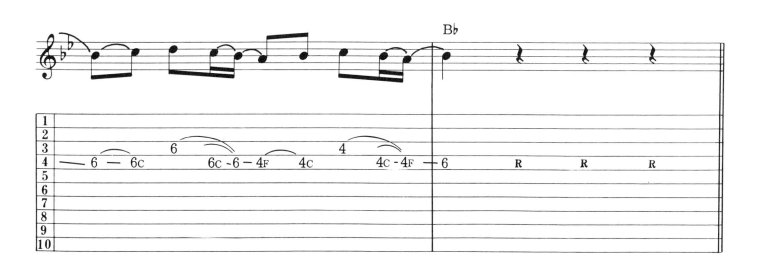

# Leather Britches

**Arranged by Doug Jernigan**
**Transcribed by Ken Albert**

Used by Permission
from "Skyhigh Steel"
Album # USR-2 Box
371 Whitehouse, Tn. 37188

**Allegro Intro**

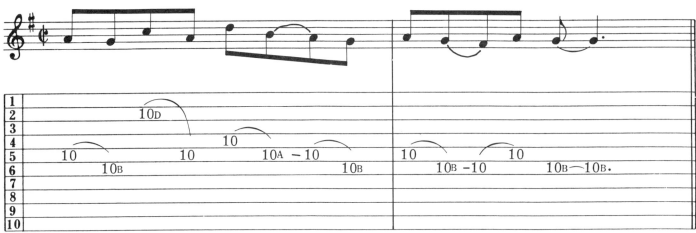

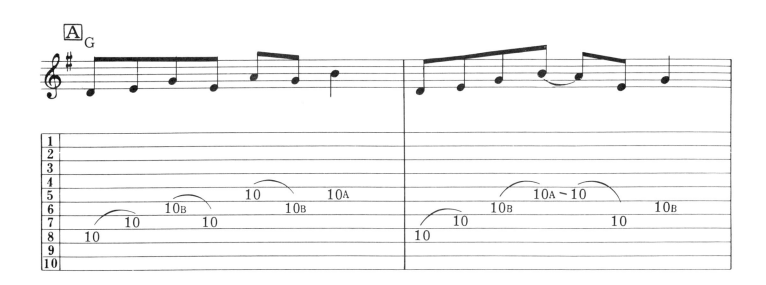

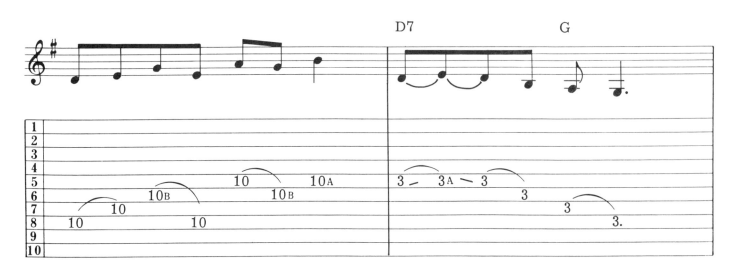

122

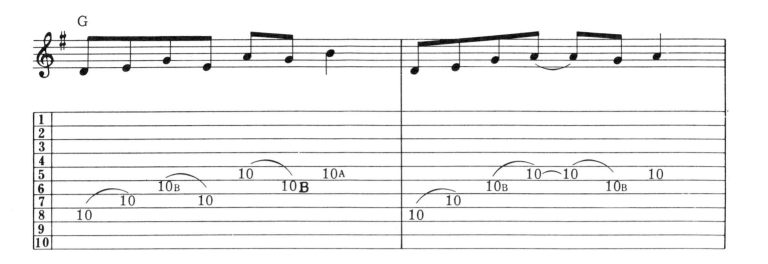

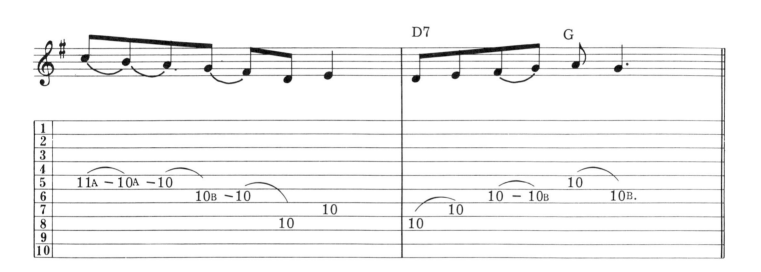

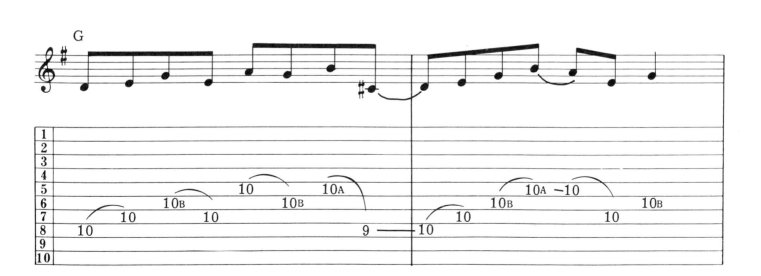

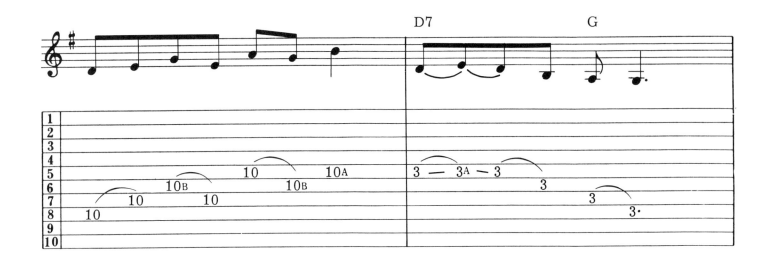

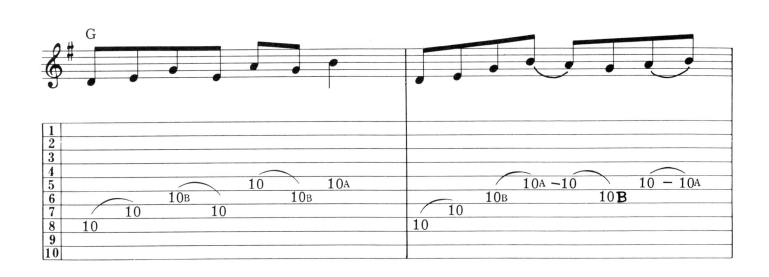

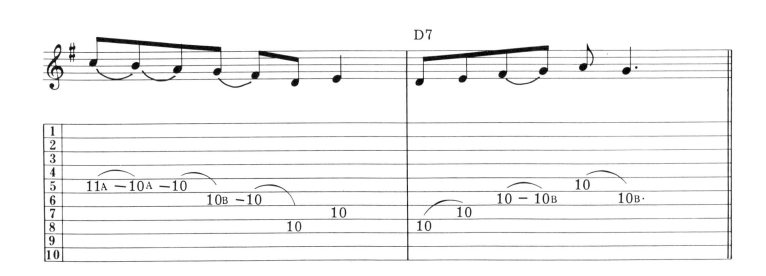

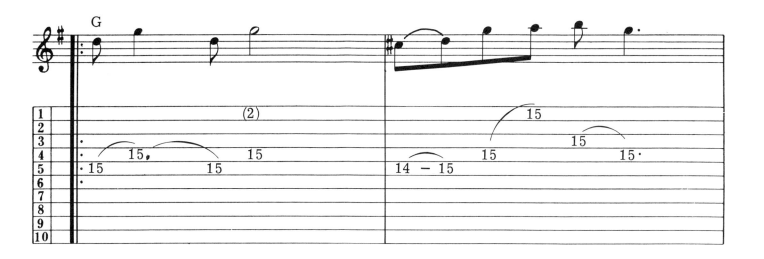

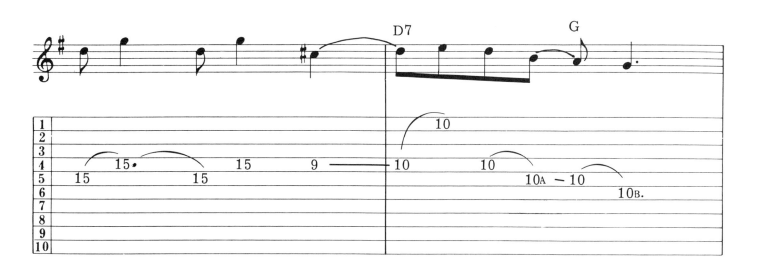

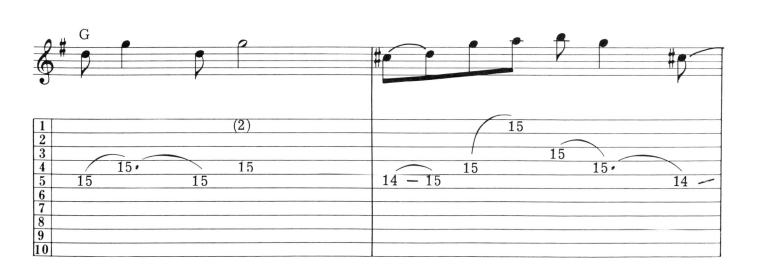

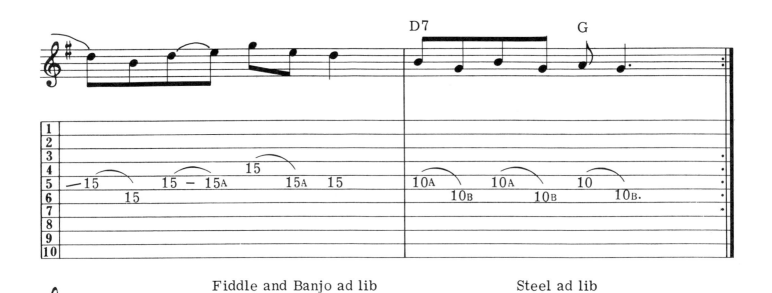

Fiddle and Banjo ad lib       Steel ad lib

24 measure rest       40 measure rest

Go back to letter **A** play thru again and then add the ending

ENDING

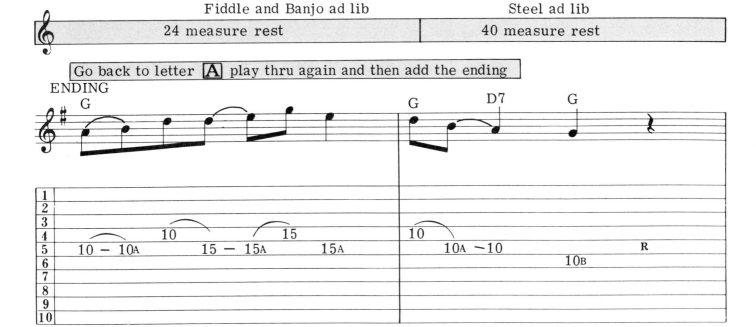

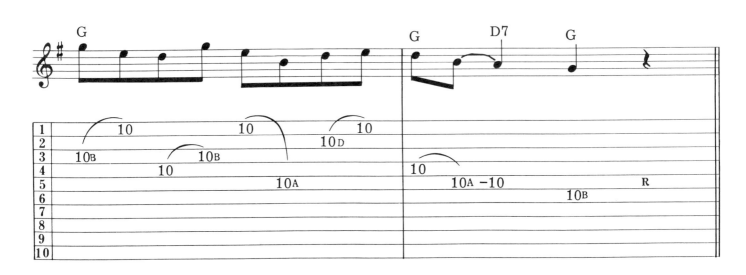

**Tom Brumley**

**Bob Maickel**

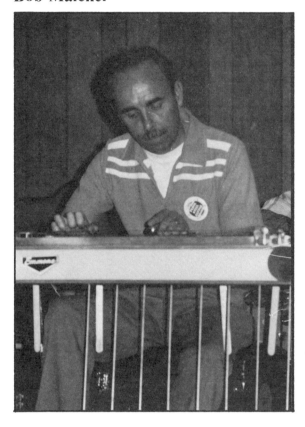

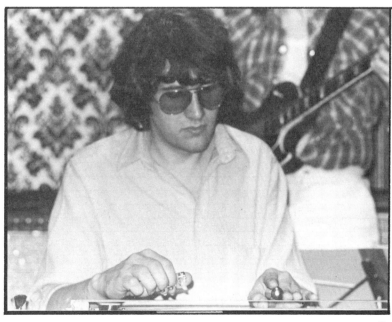

**Jean Yves Lozach**
*–France*

127

# Doug's Melody
## Knee Lever D

by Doug Jernigan
Transcribed by Ken Albert

Used with Permission
from Skyhigh Steel Album
USR-2 PO Box 467 White House,
Tn. 37188

D= Lower whole tone
D½= Lower half tone

**Moderato**

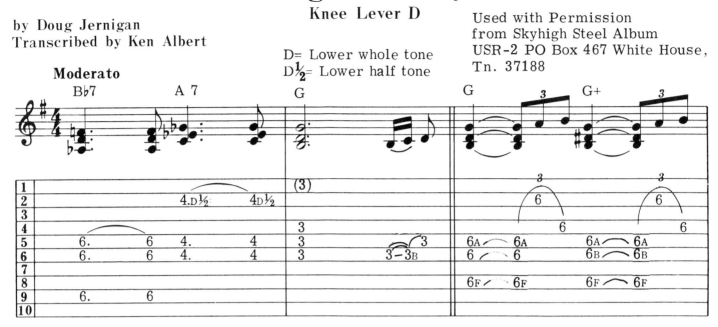

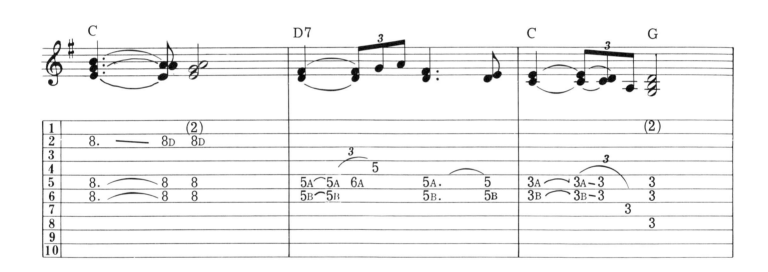

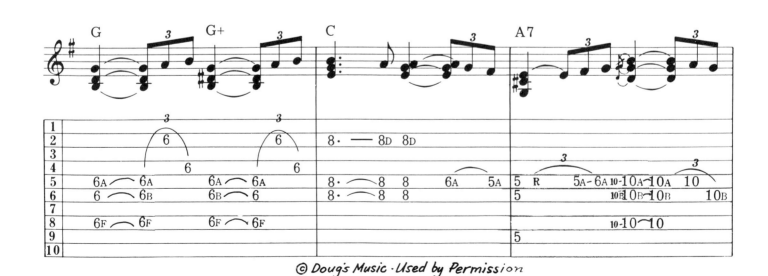

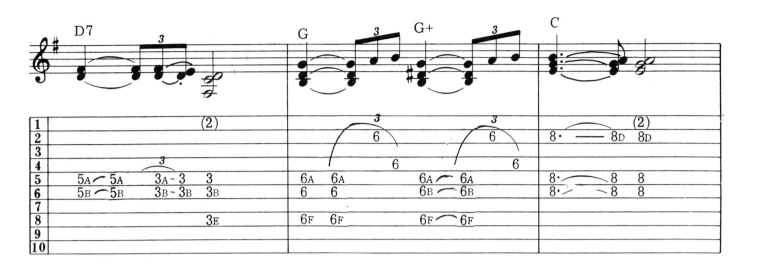

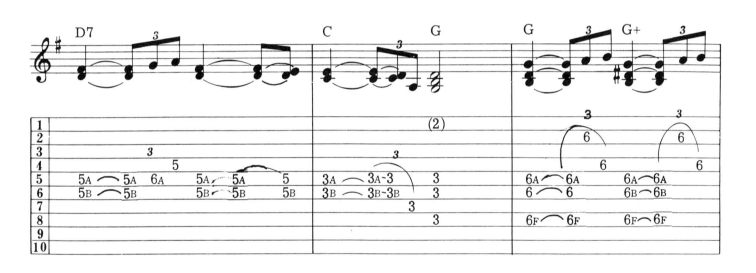

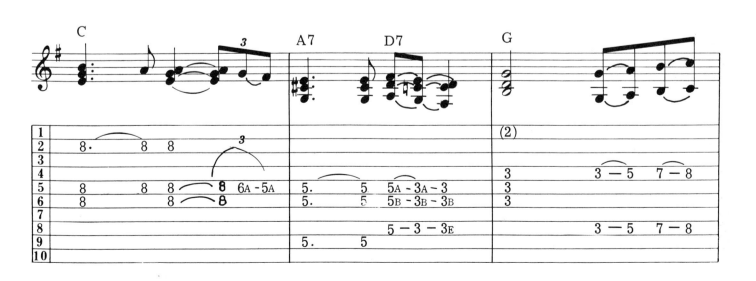

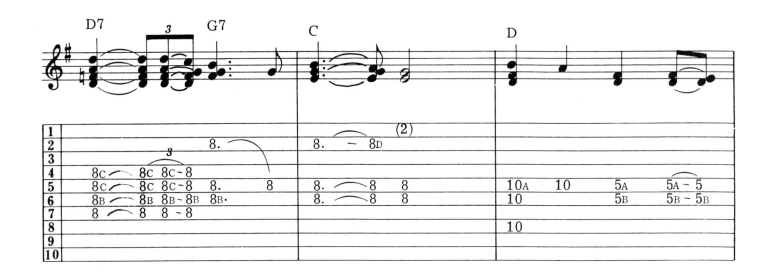

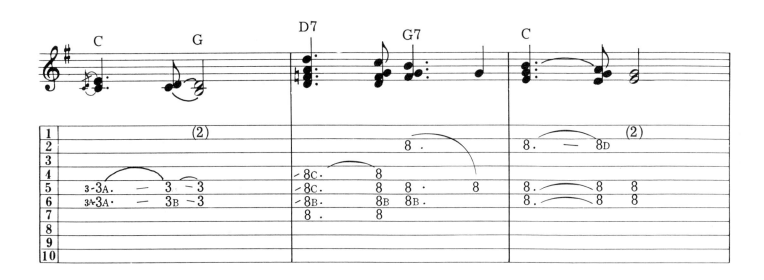

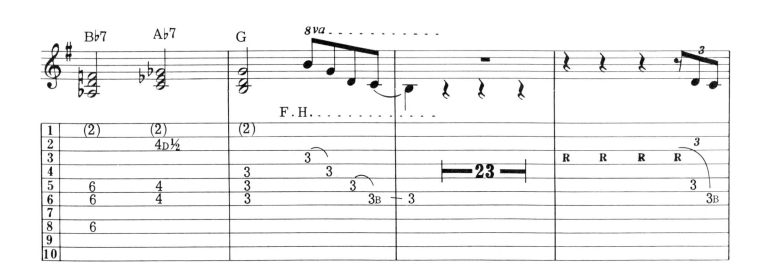

130

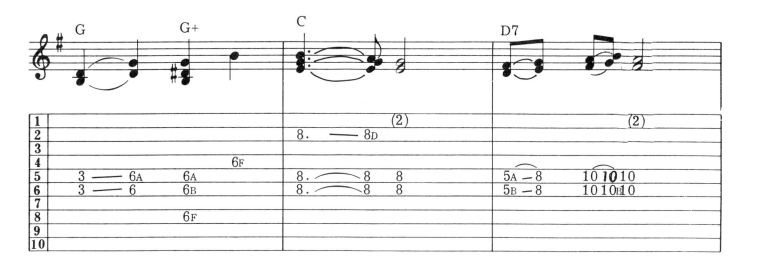

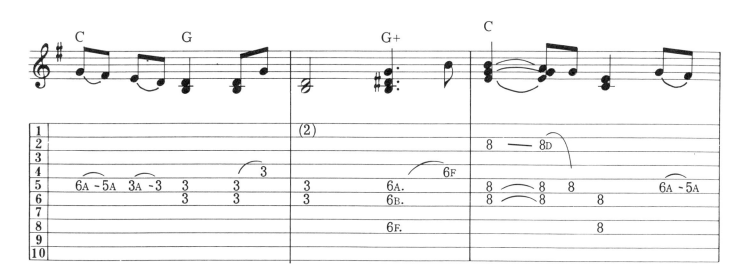

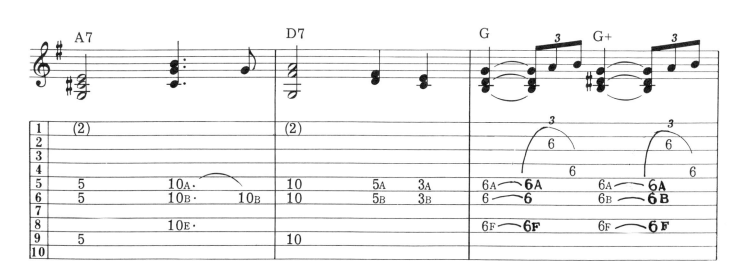

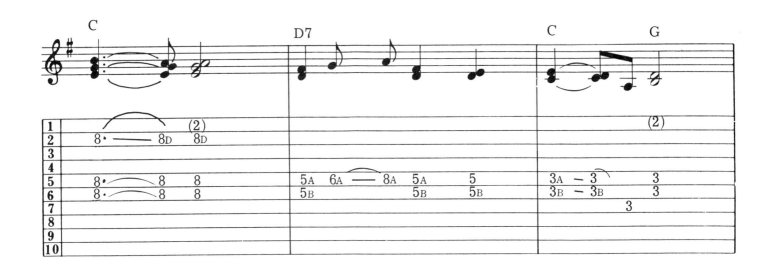

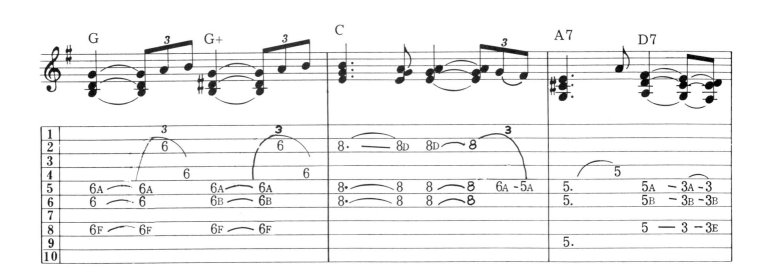

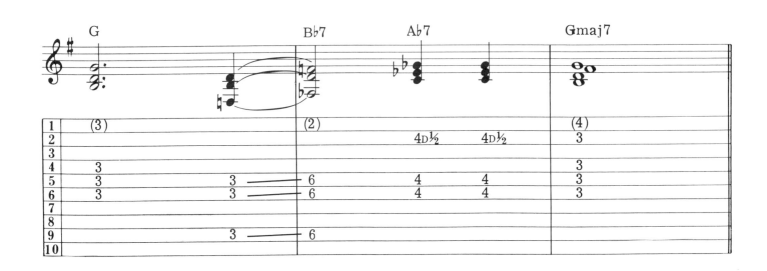

**Jerry Garcia**

**Bobby Black**

**Frank Baum**
*—Germany*

133

# Song For Sara

**Music by Paul Franklin**

Used with permission from
the album "Just Pickin" MD-26
Mid-land Records 9535
Midland;St. Louis, Mo. 63114

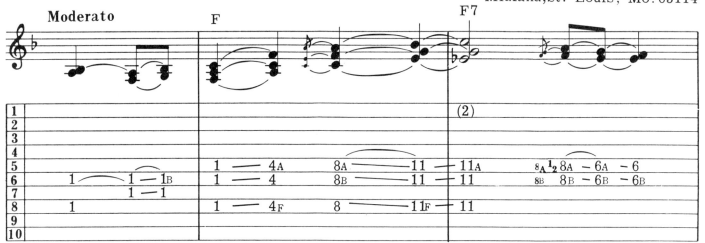

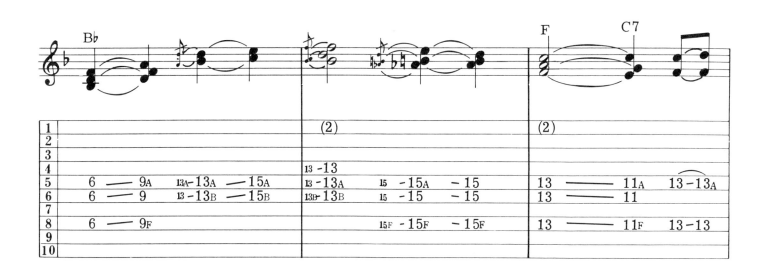

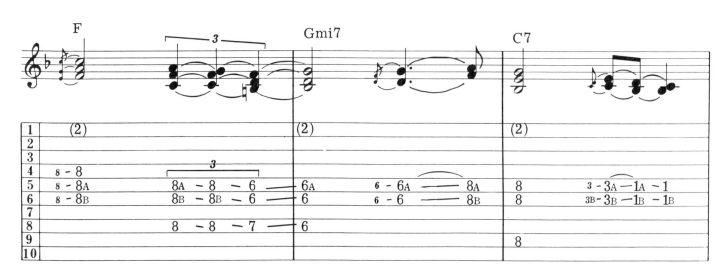

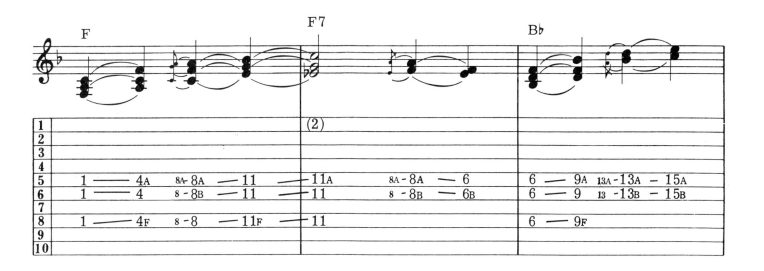

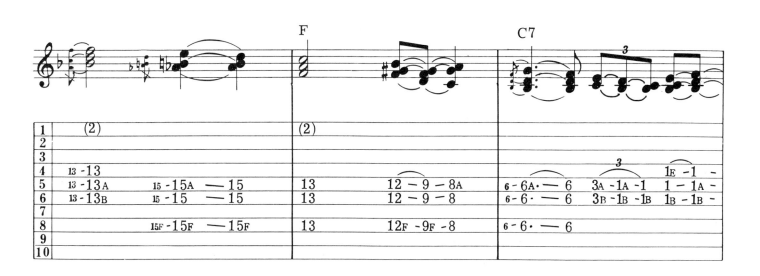

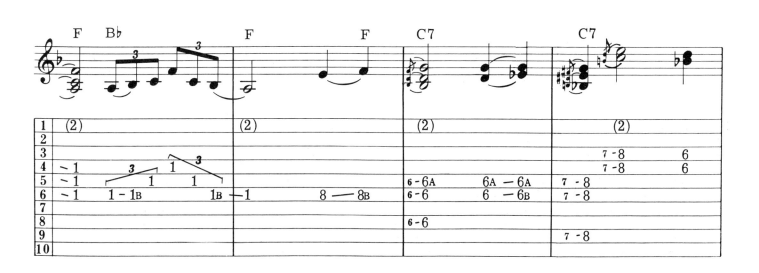

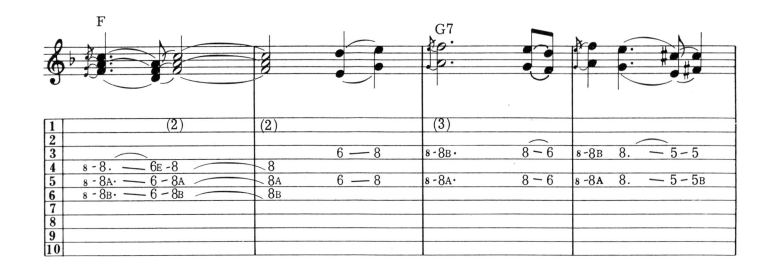

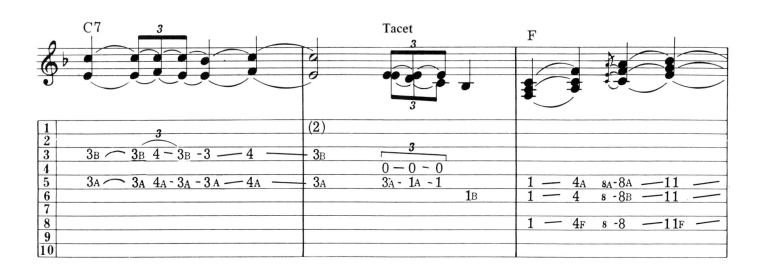

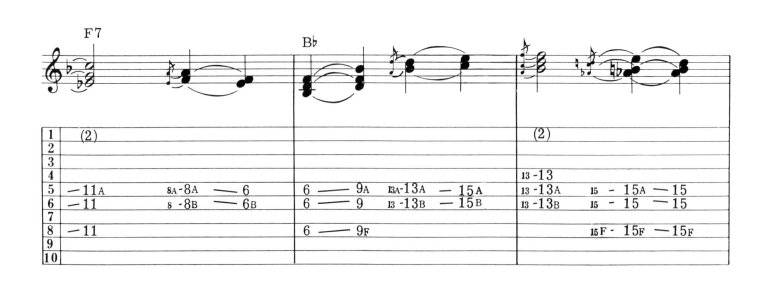

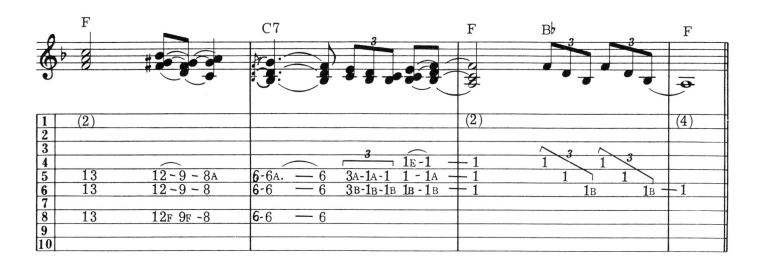

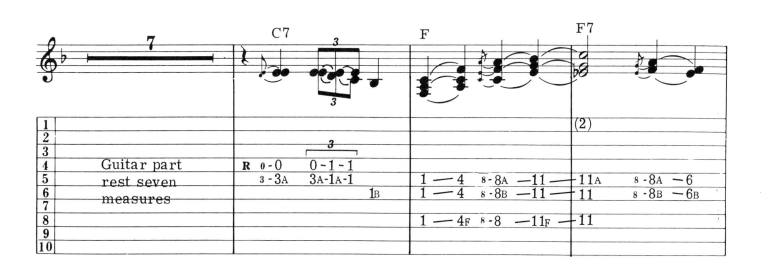

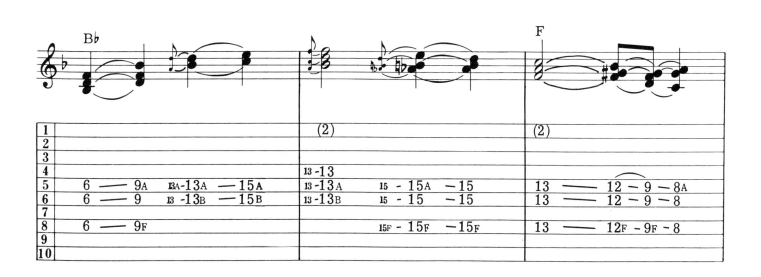

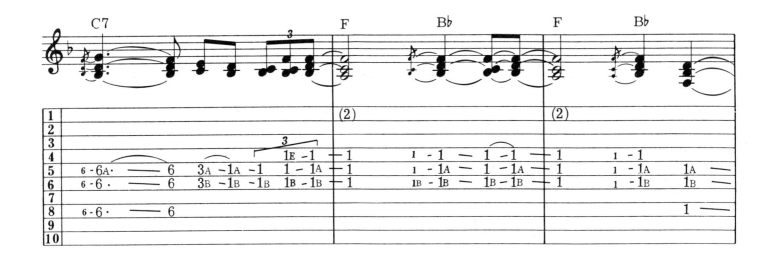

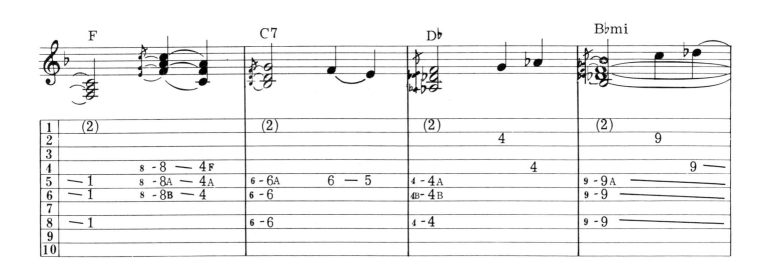

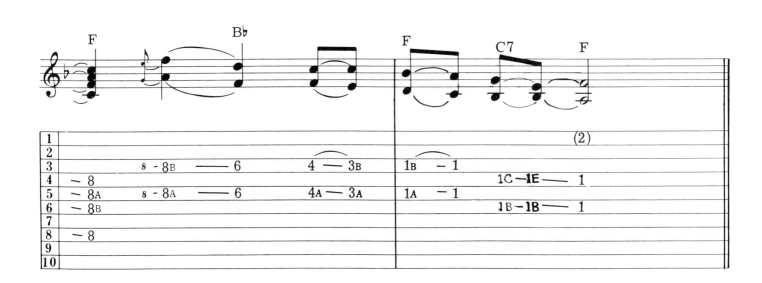

**Kayton Roberts**

**Hank Corwin**

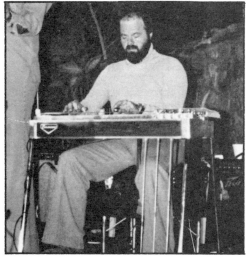

**Frans Doolaard**
*–Holland*

# Reminiscing

by Jerry Byrd

Used with Permission Combine Music Co.
from the Album "Admirable Byrd"
Monument MLP 8014

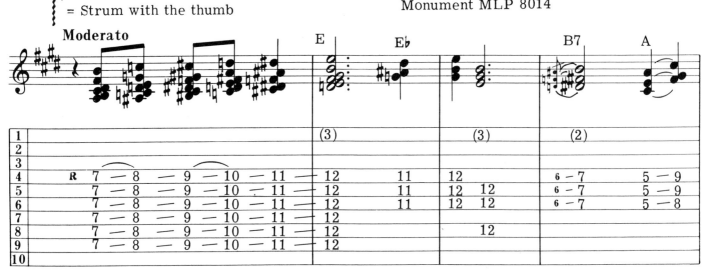

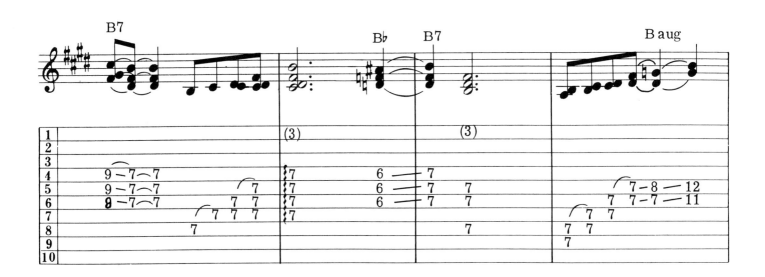

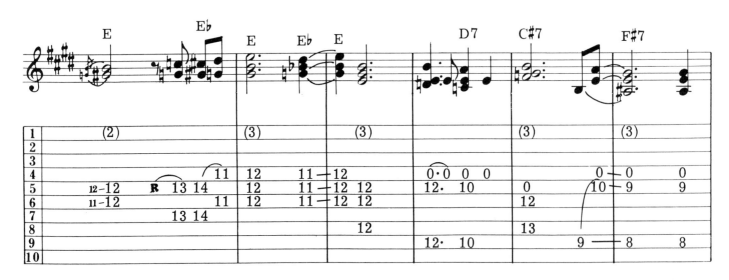

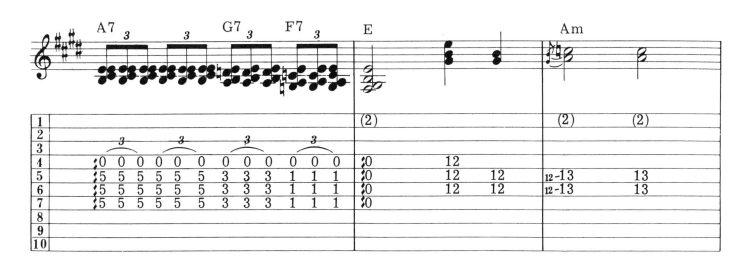

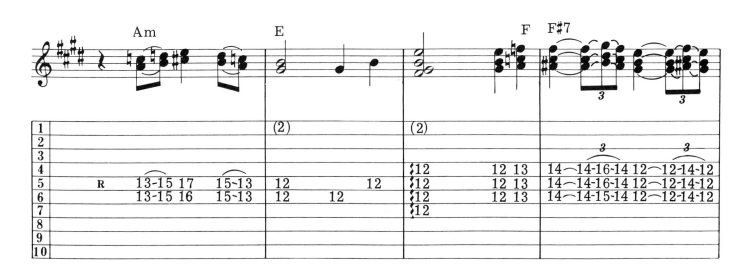

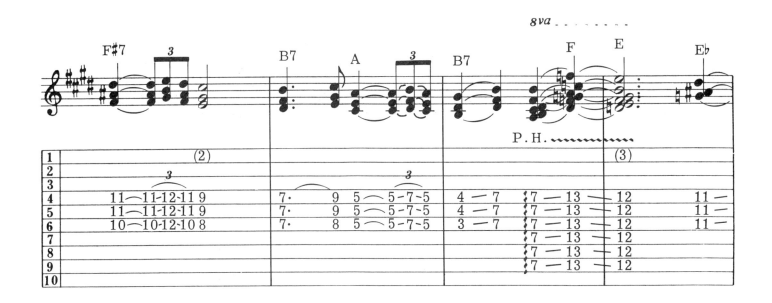

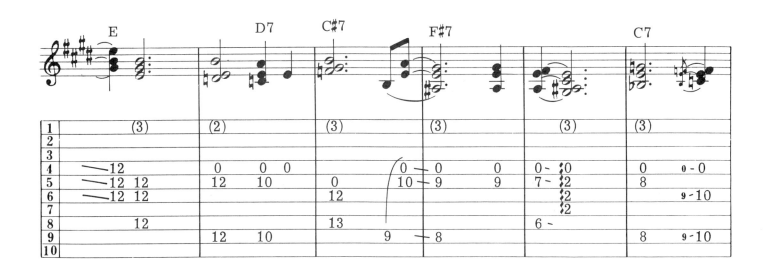

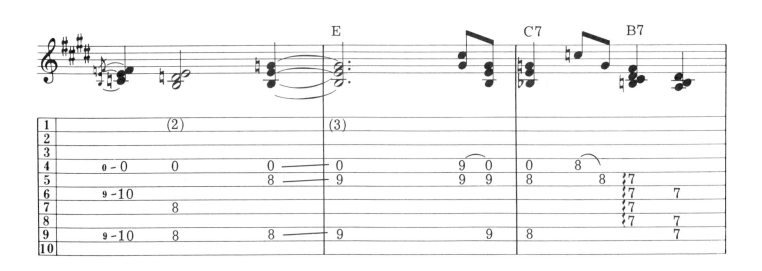

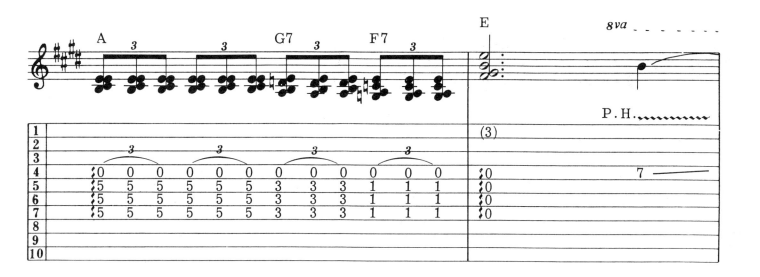

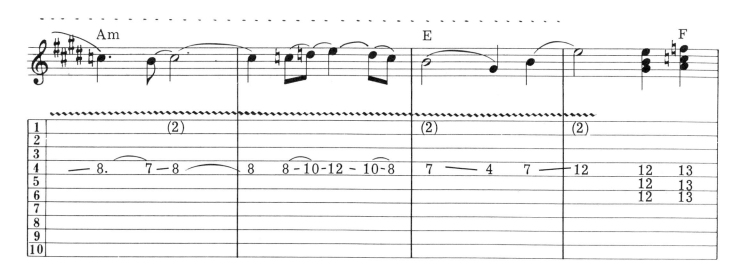

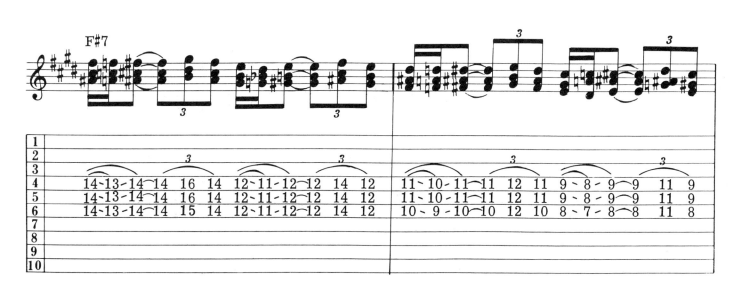

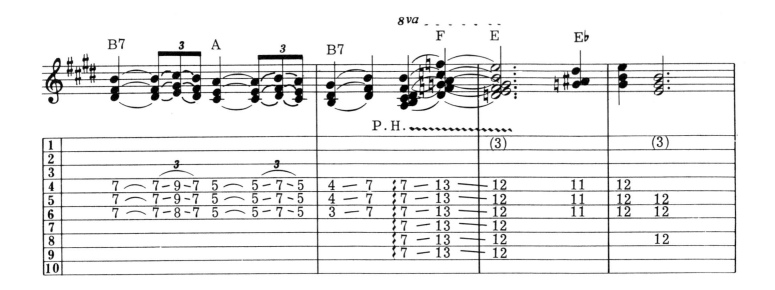

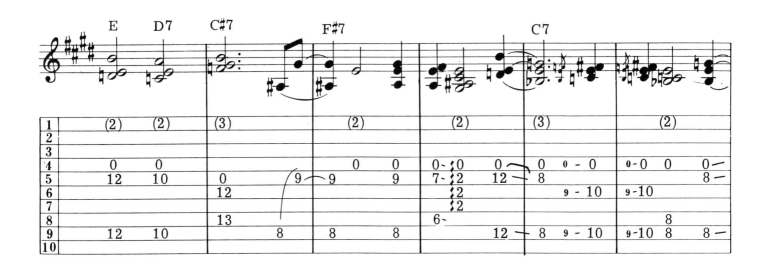

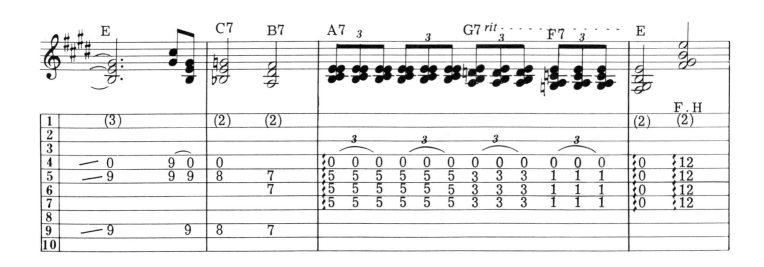

**Jimmy Crawford**

**Larry Sasser**

**John Call**

# Blue Jade

by Buddy Emmons

Used by Permission from the album "Buddy Emmons" live in St. Louis #1SGC-3 Mid-land Records P.O. Box 2581 St. Louis, Mo. 63114

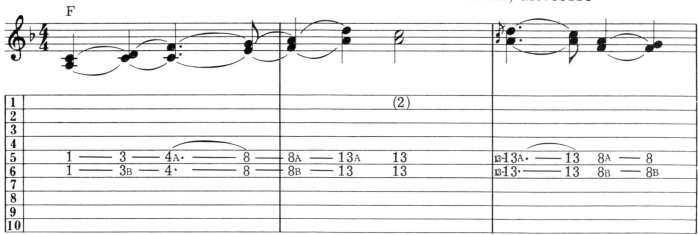

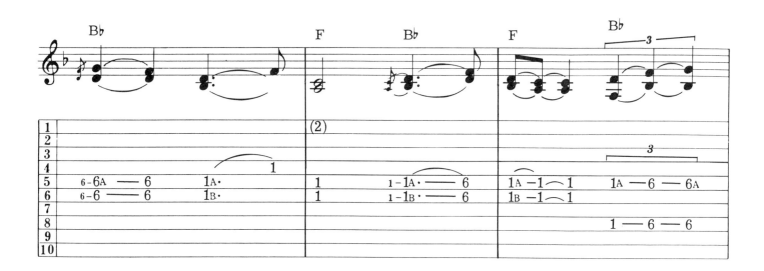

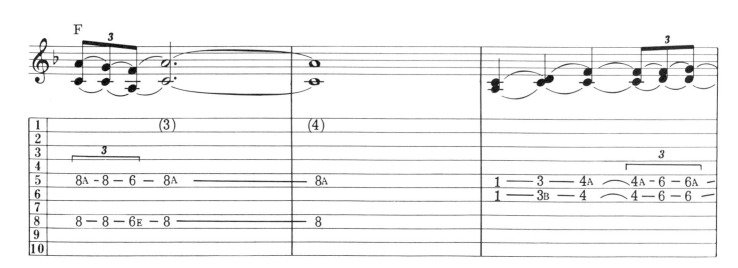

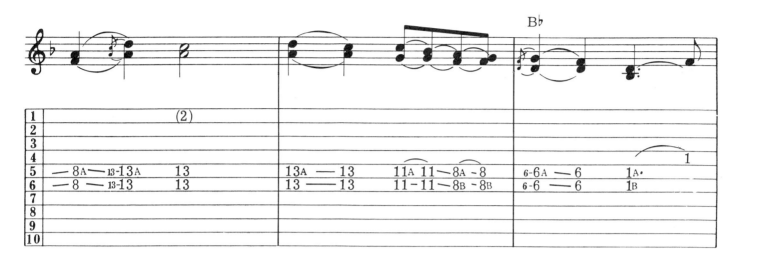

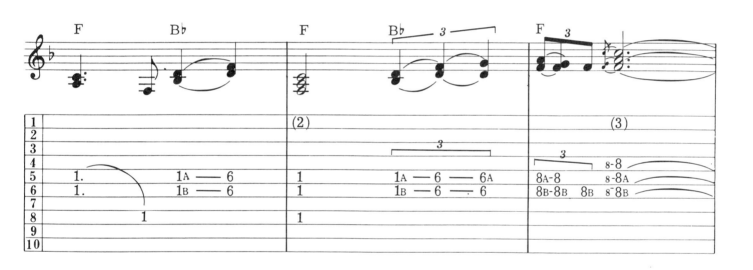

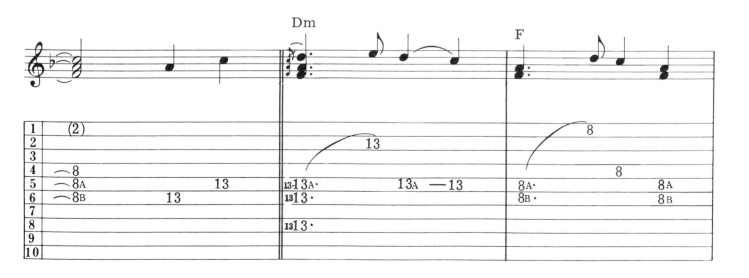

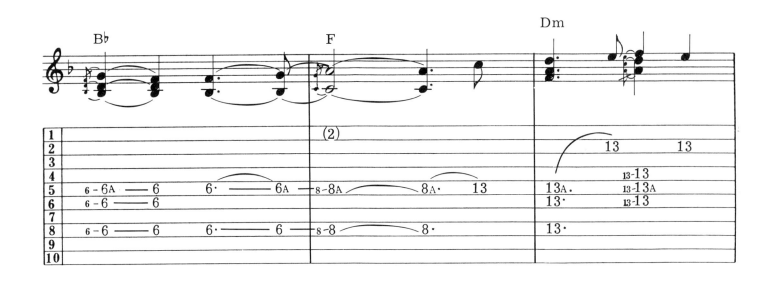

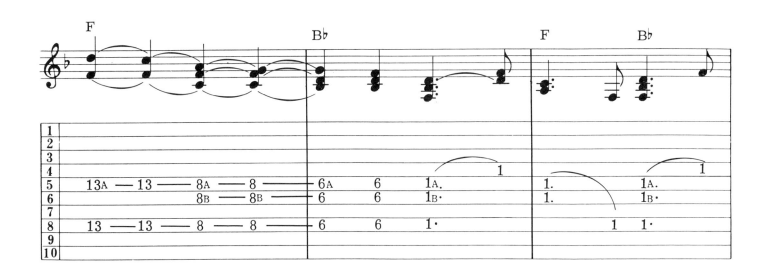

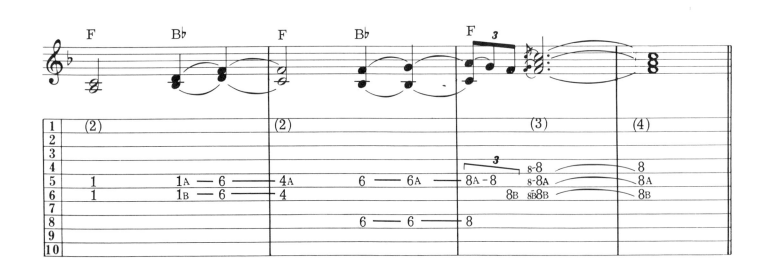

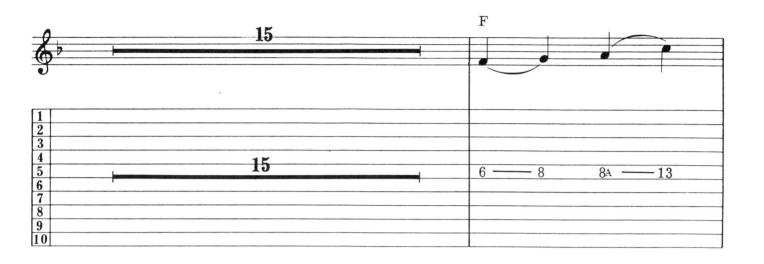

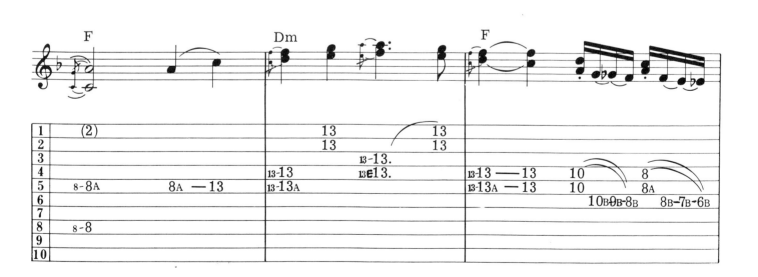

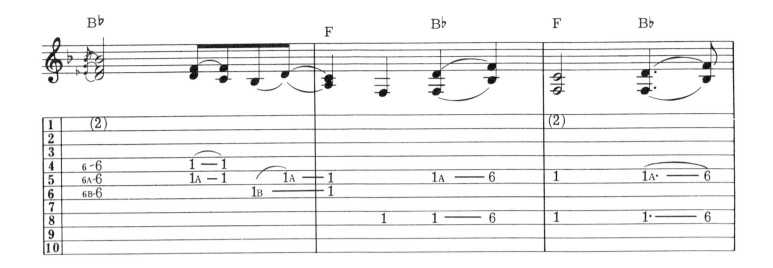

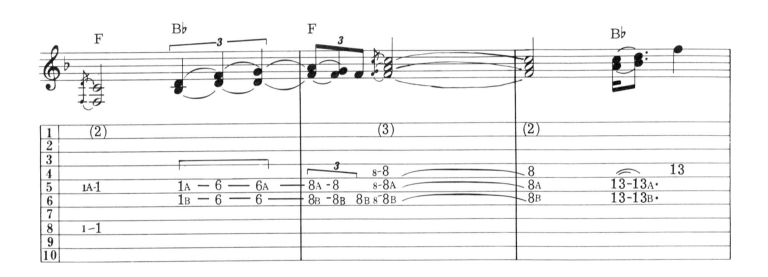

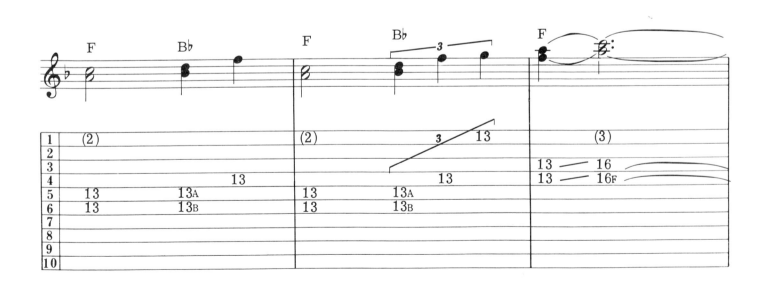

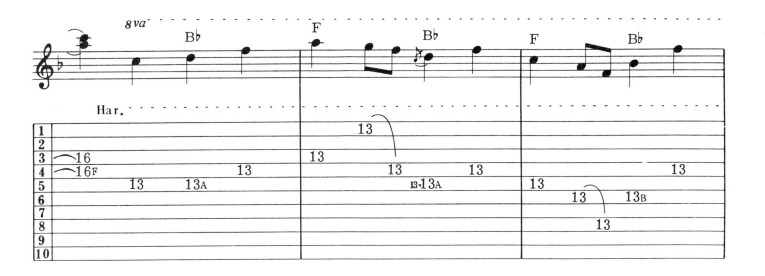

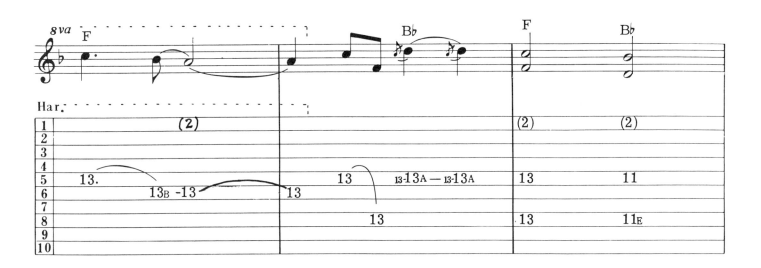

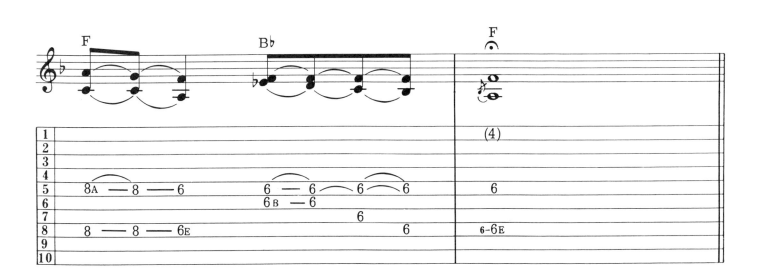

**Herbie Wallace**

**Eric Johs Lind** –*Denmark*

**Sonny Curtis**

**Claude Samard**
–*France*

**Terry Bethel**

**Al Brisco**
*—Canada*

153

**Bobbe Seymour**

**Julian Tharpe**

**Katz**
**Kobayashi** *–Japan*

**Joaquin Murphy**

**Zane Beck**

154

**B. J. Cole**  *England*

**Carl Kaye**
*–Austria*

**Buddy Charlton**

**Harold "Shot" Jackson**

**Nils Tuxen**
*–Denmark*

**Herb Remington**

**Sneaky Pete Kleinow**

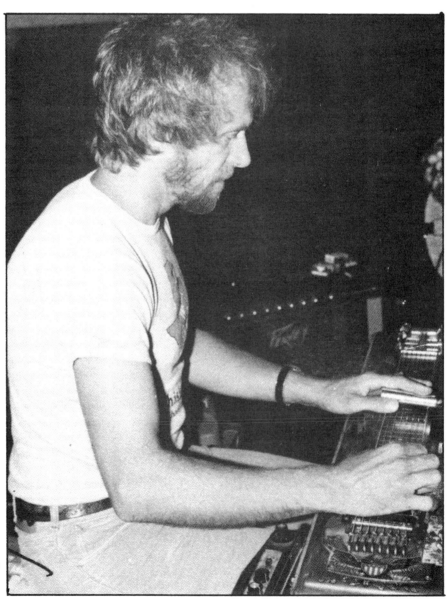

**Georges Chatagny**
*–Switzerland*

**Doug Jernigan**

**Jim Molberg**
*—New Zealand*

**Wally Murphy**

**Russ Wever**

**Michael Keane**

*Ireland*

**Norm Bodkin**
*—Australia*

**Barbara Mandrell**

**Lucky Oceans**

**Stu Basore**

**Red Saxon**
*Germany*

**Howard White**

159

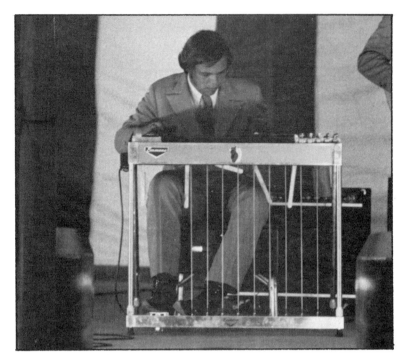

**Bob Hempker**

**Randy Beavers**